Hurricane Girl

Hurricane Girl

THE LIFE AND CAREER OF PIONEER AIRWOMAN, WINIFRED CROSSLEY

JAMES BROWN

Pen & Sword
AVIATION

First published in Great Britain in 2026 by
PEN AND SWORD AVIATION
An imprint of
Pen & Sword Books Limited
Yorkshire – Philadelphia

ISBN 978 1 03619 793 3

A CIP catalogue record for this book is available from the British Library.

Typeset in Ehrhardt 11/14 by
SJmagic DESIGN SERVICES, India.
Printed and bound in the UK by CPI Group (UK) Ltd, Croydon, CR0 4YY.

The Publisher's authorised representative in the EU for product safety is
Authorised Rep Compliance Ltd., Ground Floor, 71 Lower Baggot Street, Dublin
D02 P593, Ireland. www.arccompliance.com

For a complete list of Pen & Sword titles please contact
PEN & SWORD BOOKS LIMITED
George House, Units 12 & 13, Beevor Street, Off Pontefract Road,
Barnsley, South Yorkshire, S71 1HN, England
E-mail: enquiries@pen-and-sword.co.uk
Website: www.pen-and-sword.co.uk

or

PEN AND SWORD BOOKS
1950 Lawrence Rd, Havertown, PA 19083, USA
E-mail: uspen-and-sword@casematepublishers.com
Website: www.penandswordbooks.com

Contents

Introduction

If you were to make a list of the greatest aeroplanes used by the British during the Second World War it would surely have to include the Hawker Hurricane and the Supermarine Spitfire, the fighters that won the Battle of Britain. It would be difficult to ignore the North American Mustang, the best long-range fighter of the time, or the Avro Lancaster, arguably the finest four-engine heavy bomber of the war. The de Havilland Mosquito was the leading multi-rôle aeroplane of the era. The best transport aircraft? Most people would probably say the Douglas Dakota. When it comes to trainers it's hard to look beyond the de Havilland Tiger Moth for basic training and the North American Harvard for teaching pupils to fly more advanced types.

Apart from their iconic status, what do all these aircraft have in common? They were among the many different aeroplanes flown by a tall, slim, attractive woman called Winifred Crossley, who had been smitten by the flying bug when she was living at Old Woodbury, in the Cambridgeshire village of Gamlingay where I grew up.

Flying weaves its extraordinary magic on ordinary mortals from all backgrounds and walks of life, and once you succumb to it there is no escape. I fell under its spell when I was very young; it happened to Winifred Crossley – Winnie – in 1933. We both went on to learn to fly, in my case half a century after she did.

She was taught in cold and draughty open-cockpit biplanes, equipped with only a handful of basic instruments. They had no brakes, no flaps and no radio. They could be difficult to control on the ground, especially in a crosswind. Engines were much less reliable than their modern counterparts, and students were taught as standard practice to throttle back and make each landing a glide approach. It was essential preparation for the almost inevitable engine failures and the subsequent forced landings to come.

It was quite different to the way I was taught, yet in many respects flying has not changed very much. The laws of physics that govern how and why an aeroplane flies are still the same. The clouds, the winds and the weather still present the same difficulties. The first solo, when your instructor climbs out and tells you to take off, fly a circuit and land on your own, is still a unique and unforgettable experience. Today's light aircraft are much safer than they were in the 1930s, but like every aeroplane ever built they can still kill you if you take liberties with them. They are generally a little faster than their pre-war counterparts, but you wouldn't know it because there is no impression of speed when you are flying, other than when you are near the ground: looking down from 2,000 feet the earth seems to be floating slowly by beneath your wings.

Flying is hugely rewarding and teaches you an awful lot about yourself, as well as adding a new dimension, literally, as well as metaphorically, to your life. It teaches you to be ruthlessly honest about your failings, both as a pilot and as a human being. Every flight and every landing is different, and you learn something from each one. It has often been said, and truly, that flying is for perfectionists. And long after your flying days are done, you will never look at the sky or see a weather forecast in the same way again. You may no longer be an active aviator, but you still see with a flyer's eye.

I can't remember a time when I was not obsessed with aviation, but I have to admit that I had never heard of Winifred Crossley until my father told me about a fatal aircraft crash at Old Woodbury that happened in 1938 when he was a boy and living at the nearby hamlet of Gamlingay Cinques. In the course of researching that accident I discovered Winnie and her extraordinary story.

She was born Winifred Harrisson in 1906, just over two years after man first flew. She was Winifred Crossley when she began learning to fly in late 1933, and Winifred Fair by the time she seemingly ceased flying at the end of 1945. During that time, urged on by the threat and then the reality of war, aviation advanced from canvas-covered biplanes into the jet age. When she died in 1984 men had landed on the moon, Concorde was carrying passengers at twice the speed of sound and the Space Shuttle was regularly taking astronauts into orbit around the earth.

Winnie's own flying career lasted a mere dozen years, but she crammed a lifetime's experience into them. When she decided to learn to fly it was not something that many women had ever done: only 260 women had been issued with a Royal Aero Club Aviator's Certificate since they started awarding them in 1911. When Winnie gained hers in 1934, she was one of just 65 women who earned one that year, compared to 838 men.

Once she had qualified as a pilot she became through obsessive practice a very fine aerobatic pilot, and then qualified as a commercial pilot able to fly 'for hire and reward'. In 1936 she was hired as the country's first professional female aerobatic display pilot, performing twice daily during the last major tour of Great Britain by a flying circus. Afterwards she had three years as a successful commercial pilot, becoming the first woman to tow banners and the first to tow gliders, before the outbreak of war brought the curtain down on civil aviation and the end of the first half of her flying life.

The second half was quite different. In January 1940 she was one of the first eight women pilots selected for the Women's Section of the Air Transport Auxiliary, and spent the next six years ferrying almost every aircraft used by the British during the Second World War. In 1941 she became the first woman ever to fly one of the RAF's frontline fighters. After the Air Transport Auxiliary was disbanded at the end of 1945 there is no evidence that she ever flew again. She may have done, of course – after all, absence of evidence is not evidence of absence – but if that really was the end of it then perhaps part of the reason might have been that after flying Hurricanes, Spitfires, Mustangs, Lancasters and many other military aircraft besides, anything else would seem rather tame by comparison.

Winifred Crossley had the good fortune to be one of a small, select group of pre-war pioneer women pilots, and then to be one of the women who served as ferry pilots during the Second World War, but she had the misfortune to die at the wrong time. Since she passed away many of her female contemporaries who achieved far less than she did but lived longer are now celebrated, while she is largely forgotten. I hope this book marks a small step towards redressing the balance.

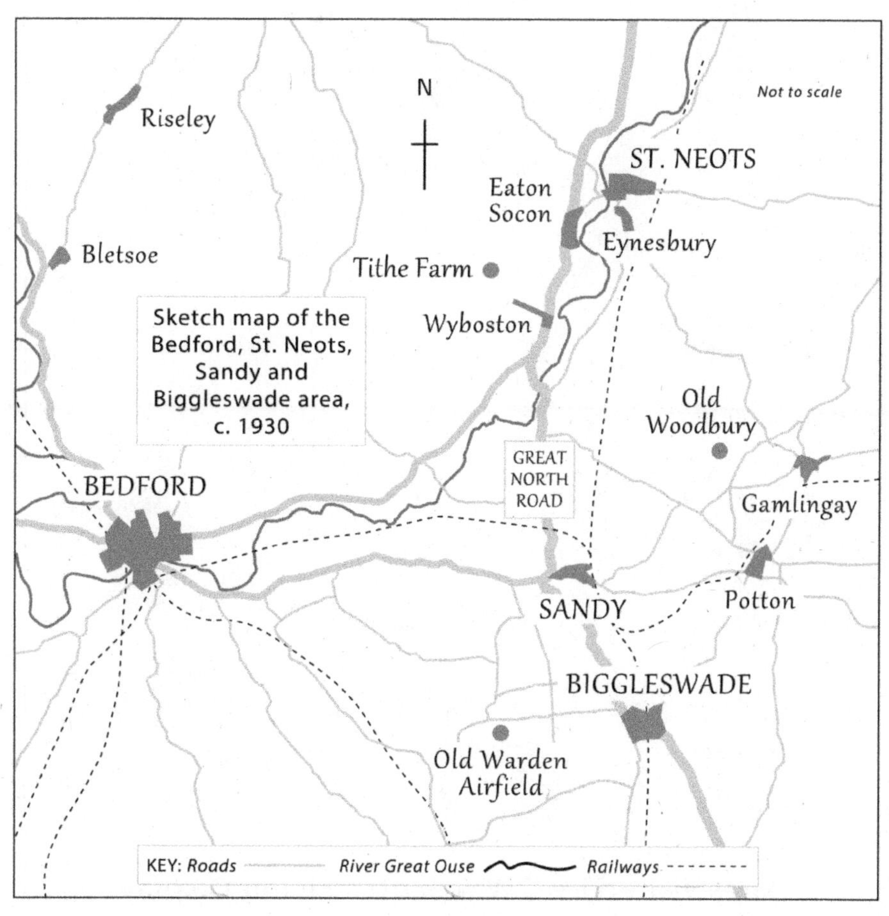

Not to scale
N
Riseley
ST. NEOTS
Eaton
Socon
Eynesbury
Bletsoe
Tithe Farm
Sketch map of the
Bedford, St. Neots,
Sandy and
Biggleswade area,
c. 1930
Wyboston
Old
Woodbury
GREAT
NORTH
ROAD
Gamlingay
BEDFORD
SANDY
Potton
BIGGLESWADE
Old Warden
Airfield
KEY: Roads   River Great Ouse   Railways

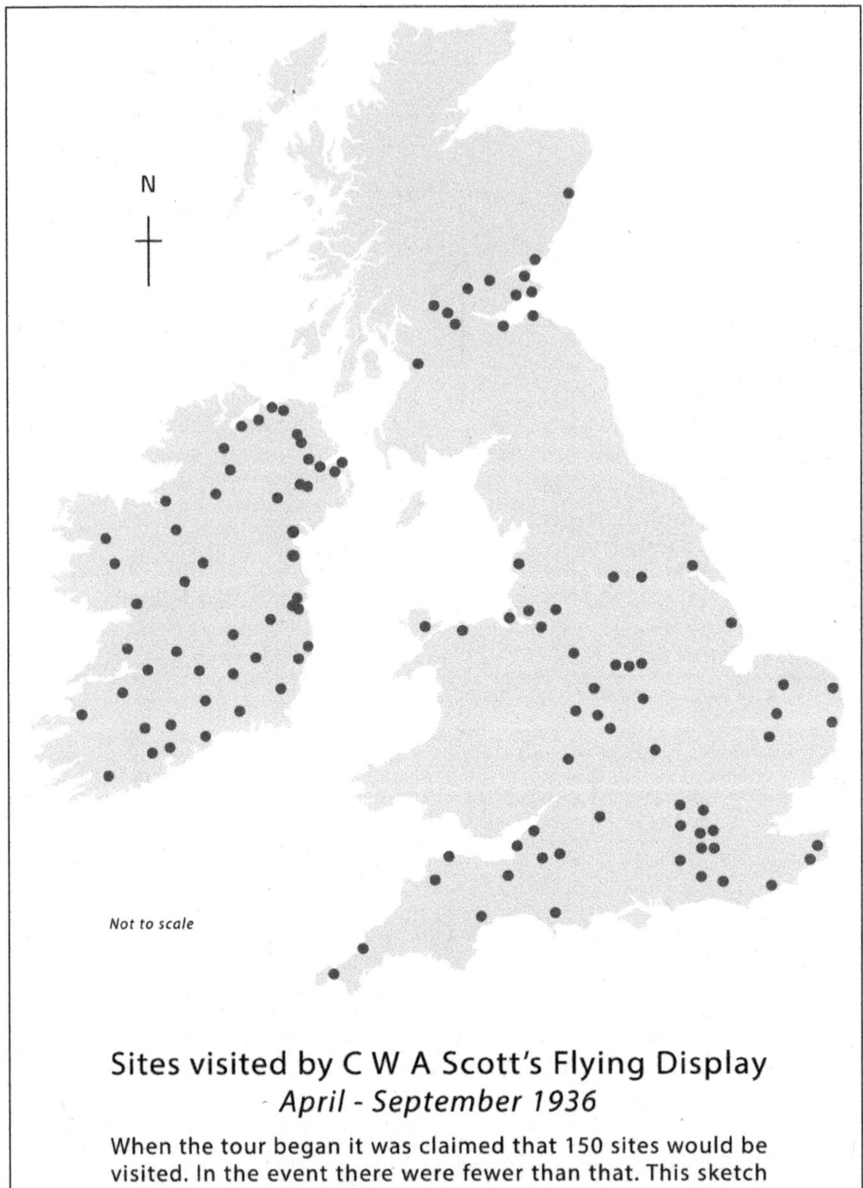

Sites visited by C W A Scott's Flying Display
April - September 1936

When the tour began it was claimed that 150 sites would be visited. In the event there were fewer than that. This sketch map shows where displays are *known* to have taken place. It clearly demonstrates the emphasis placed on touring Ireland.

Chapter One

County Set

The poet Robert Frost called it *The Road Not Taken*, that point in life most people reach sooner or later where two roads diverge and you must choose which one to travel on. What seems like a trivial decision at the time can often be seen in retrospect to have had profound – even life-changing – consequences. For 27-year-old Mrs. Winifred Crossley, of Old Woodbury in Gamlingay, the decisive moment came in the summer of 1933. It may have happened at Huntingdon on 30 May or at Cambridge on 1 June, but the chances are that it took place on Tuesday, 13 June 1933 at Tythe Farm in Wyboston, a village on the Great North Road near St. Neots.

The occasion was the visit of Sir Alan Cobham's National Aviation Day flying display. Popularly known as 'Cobham's Flying Circus' the displays were hugely successful events, and gave many thousands of people their first experience of flying. Indeed, the first season in 1932 was so successful that in 1933 Cobham ran two simultaneous tours, known prosaically as Number One and Number Two tours. It was the Number One tour that had displayed at Huntingdon and Cambridge, but it was the Number Two tour that visited Wyboston on 13 June 1933 having displayed at Tamworth the day before.

Like all of Cobham's shows, the one in Wyboston had been well-publicised in advance with posters and announcements and advertisements in the local press, all proclaiming the exciting arrival of the 'Great Air Display' on its summer tour. Cobham was a pioneer pilot, part showman and part crusader, who had achieved fame and a knighthood for his record-breaking, long-distance flights. The National Aviation Day displays he created in 1932 combined barnstorming thrills and spills with joyriding, and visited hundreds of sites around the country, many of which were nothing more than farmers' fields cleared for the purpose.

Two complete displays were scheduled at each venue, those at Wyboston starting at a quarter to three in the afternoon and at seven in the evening. The publicity promised they would 'depict all that is finest in aircraft and piloting skill', in a programme that included a parachutist 'taking a header into space', wingwalking, formation aerobatics and a 'sensational exhibition of crazy flying'. To further entertain the spectators who forked out 1s. 3d. each to see the show there was to be a 'fearless display of upside-down flying by a famous pilot' as well as 'trapeze acrobatics at a height of seven hundred feet'.

As if all that wasn't exciting enough, the public were also promised the opportunity to take to the air themselves, with passenger flights available from four shillings. According to the *Bedfordshire Times and Independent*, despite the unsettled weather a large number of people attended both displays, with the passenger flights doing good business, while 'several adventurous people tasted the thrills of looping the loop and of other "stunts"'.

Given her subsequent career, it's likely that Winnie Crossley was one of those adventurous people. She was not the sort of person who would have been content with a hasty circuit when, for a few shillings more, she could experience the sensations of a couple of loops and a spin.

It's probable that she had more than one flight that day: she later told a journalist that it was going up for *flights* with Cobham that gave her the flying bug. She told another reporter in 1936 that 'I visited an air display, and after that decided to become a pilot'. She added 'I have never regretted the decision'. Whether she knew it or not at the time, she had chosen the road she would take from then on.

* * *

Winnie was born Winifred Mary Harrisson on 9 January 1906 in St. Neots, Huntingdonshire, along with her twin sister Daphne Louisa. Their parents were Ernest and Winifred Harrisson. The twins had an elder brother, John, known as Jack, who was born in 1904, and they would eventually be joined by two younger siblings, George who arrived in 1909, and Muriel, born in 1912.

Winnie's maternal grandfather was a captain in the Royal Navy and her Harrisson grandfather was a well-to-do miller and farmer in Holbeach in Lincolnshire. Her father Ernest was one of six brothers, four of whom went up to Cambridge, although one brother died before he could graduate. Two of the Harrisson brothers became doctors, and two qualified as solicitors. Ernest studied medicine, graduating from Clare College. In 1903 he went into partnership with another doctor in St. Neots in Huntingdonshire, married, and settled down to life as a general practitioner in a small market town.

Yet Dr. E.H. Harrisson was a cut above the average country medical man, socially superior to most of his patients and with a lifestyle and income which gave the family almost automatic membership of that now-vanished group of people known as 'the county set'. The Harrissons' homes in St. Neots proclaimed as much. To begin with the family lived in The Priory, a pleasant enough place with a garden that backed on to the River Great Ouse; according to the 1911 Census it boasted fourteen rooms, 'not including the dispensary', and three live-in servants. Shortly before the First World War the Harrissons moved to the altogether grander surroundings of The Shrubbery. This was a large, comfortable L-shaped house next door to St. Mary's Church, with high walls and a gated entrance on to Church Street, and grounds big enough to need the services of a gardener. Dr. Harrisson and his wife would spend the rest of their married life there.

Details of Winnie's childhood and adolescence are notable mainly for their absence. She later stated that she had been educated at Burchett House School in Dorking, Surrey. There are a handful of references to the school in the local press, all dating from between 1915 and 1918, which indicate that Burchett House was a girls' boarding school run by Miss Amy Watson. By 1921 Winnie and her twin sister Daphne were at another boarding school for girls, this one in East Finchley.

The education on offer is unlikely to have been much different from that taught in countless other similar establishments at the time. It was fairly basic, perhaps with a little French thrown in, and lessons on elocution and deportment, along with the development of whatever musical talents a pupil might have. The aim was to produce young girls whose only goal in life was to get married, after which they would be content to play a subordinate role as the perfect wife and mother. The idea of a woman having a career, or indeed any kind of independent life, was not a consideration.

The first time Winnie is noted in the press she is already nineteen and probably living at home in St. Neots. Along with her twin sister Daphne and her elder brother Jack, she belonged to what the *Biggleswade Chronicle* in its issue of 24 April 1925 described as 'a party of amateur artistes' from St. Neots calling themselves 'The Kute Kids', who put on a show at the Victory Cinema in Sandy to raise money for some new tennis courts, bowling greens and a croquet lawn at the Conservative Club in the town. The first part of the show was presented as a variety bill, during which Winnie, among other appearances on the stage, gave the audience *I Makes 'Em Do The Cake Walk*, in which she was assisted by Mr. Surtees Wilkinson and Mr. Frank Crossley. The second part of the show took the form of a three-act comedy burlesque called *Algy Throws An Indiscretion*. All three Harrisson siblings took part in it, as did Mr. Frank Crossley.

Sandy's new sports facilities were officially opened in July 1925. The *Biggleswade Chronicle* noted that the tennis tournament was comfortably won by Winifred Harrisson and Frank Crossley.

***

Frank Crossley – James Francis Crossley to give him his full name – was born on 20 August 1905, the son of Bertram Crossley from the Derbyshire mining and industrial town of Ripley. Frank's great-grandfather James Crossley had established a mill in Ripley in 1852 to manufacture lamp, stove and candle wicks. The business passed to his son James junior, and after his death in 1903, to Frank's father Bertram in turn. Soon afterwards the firm amalgamated with two other similar firms to become Morgan Crossley, which claimed to be the biggest supplier of wicks in the world.

Bertram Crossley was 22 when he married Isabella Coulson in 1904, but she died in 1906, perhaps from complications following Frank's birth. Bertram Crossley was an enthusiastic member of the local Territorial Army, and shortly after the outbreak of war in August 1914 he was transferred to The Sherwood Foresters. His health broke down during training and he resigned his commission, always regretting that he was unable to go on active service with his battalion. He remarried in 1916 but died suddenly at home in January 1918, at the age of 36. His death certificate gave the cause of death as epilepsy and his occupation as a retired cotton manufacturer. He had presumably been epileptic most of his life. Although he retained his place on the board of Morgan Crossley he had probably not been active in the business because of his health.

Frank grew up never knowing his mother, and the ill-health, second marriage and early death of his father suggest that he probably did not have an easy childhood. Like many other boys at the end of the First World War, he found himself without a father to guide him.

The Crossleys were a wealthy family and at least there was no shortage of money. Frank attended Malvern College, a public school founded in 1865 in the Worcestershire spa town of Malvern. The pages of the school magazine, *The Malvernian*, record that he represented the school at both cricket and football. A photograph of the Malvern football team appeared in the *Illustrated Sporting and Dramatic News* in 1922, in which J.F. Crossley, a slight, thin-faced boy with prominent cheekbones, hands thrust into the pockets of his shorts, stares blankly at the camera.

After leaving Malvern, Frank went up to Pembroke College, Cambridge, where he obtained a Bachelor of Arts degree. He played football for the University against the army in 1923. By 1925 he was playing tennis with Winnie Harrisson, but how, where and when they first met is not known. Somewhere along the line romance blossomed and on 8 September 1926 in St. Neots parish church, which adjoined the Harrissons' family home at The Shrubbery, she and Frank were married. They left the reception at 4 pm for London, from where they were to fly to Italy for their honeymoon.

* * *

On their return Mr. and Mrs. Crossley stayed for a few months in the village of Bletsoe in the north Bedfordshire countryside, some ten miles west of St. Neots. In February 1927 they spent £1,600 on purchasing the lease of a detached five-bedroom house 3 miles away on the outskirts of the village of Riseley. It was called The Mallowry, set in three acres of land at the end of a long drive and surrounded by farmland. It had been built a couple of decades earlier in Cape Dutch Colonial style, a wide, whitewashed house with a long roof, tall chimneys and shutters on the upstairs windows. Inside were three large and elegant reception rooms, with a fine staircase leading up to a long gallery on the first floor. Outside, in addition to the gardens, lawns, trees and shrubs, there was a tennis court.

The brief glimpses we have of Frank's school and university career suggest he was sporty rather than academic. The Harrissons were also a sporty lot. Two of Winnie's uncles played Minor Counties cricket for Lincolnshire and football for Holbeach. All the Harrissons played golf: Winnie played the game all her life. Her father Dr. Harrisson was a member of St. Neots Golf Club and sometimes played with his son-in-law Frank Crossley in matches against other clubs in the area. Frank himself won the St. Neots Golf Club's Steward's Cup in 1929. Winnie's younger brother George captained the St. Neots' golfers in the 1930s, and played at a sufficiently high standard to take part in the 1946 English Amateur Championship, the first to be held after the Second World War. He played cricket alongside Frank Crossley and Lord Malden in the Gentlemen of Huntingdonshire team which took on the Old Modernians in 1928.

Cricket, golf and tennis are sports which each require specific clothing and equipment, dedicated facilities, membership of a club or clubs and plenty of free time in which to play. Most ordinary folk possessed neither the money nor the leisure to indulge in them. Golf and tennis were the preserve of the upper middle classes who derived most of their income from investments and did not have to undertake daily work (presumably Frank derived at least some of his income from the shares in Morgan Crossley; he does not seem to have had an actual job).

George Orwell described this group as 'an entirely functionless class... the people whose photographs you can look at in the *Tatler* and the *Bystander*, always supposing that you want to'. Winnie was to appear several times in both publications, but what seems to be the first photograph of her in the press appeared in the pages of *The Sketch* on 30 November 1927 in a report on the Pytchley Hunt's meet at Cottesbrooke in Northamptonshire. Taken little more than a year after her marriage, the photographer has captured Mrs. Frank Crossley standing on a stile along with three other ladies, their excited grins and exaggerated attention focused on the invisible Hunt. Each is wearing a fashionable cloche hat, their eyes barely discernible beneath the rim. Winnie has on a fur coat with a large collar, gloves, silk stockings and court shoes. She clutches a handbag in her left hand, and if not exactly dressed for following the Hunt she looks every inch the liberated flapper.

The Crossleys themselves may well have hunted. Their chestnut gelding Flash won the 'Hack of Hunter Type' class at the 1928 County Agricultural Show held in Bedford, and the nearby Oakley Hunt is known to have met at least once at The Mallowry while they lived there. Frank won numerous prizes for his fruit, vegetables and flowers at the Riseley show each year but it was the couple's prowess at tennis that was most often reflected in the sports reports of the local papers.

Having their own court to practice on must have been a great advantage. They took part in local tournaments and those held further afield in places like Cromer and Hunstanton. Both Frank and Winnie were good enough to represent Bedfordshire, and photographs survive of Frank with the men's team and of the tall, attractive, athletic-looking Winnie with the women's team.

From the outside at least, life for the Crossleys seems to have consisted largely of filling the endless hours of leisure their income gave them with the traditional country pursuits of their time and class. The birth of their son John James Crossley in early 1929 seems barely to have ruffled the calm waters of their existence, and life went on much as before.

Towards the end of 1932 the Crossleys left Riseley, although oddly they seem to have retained the lease of The Mallowry until 1935. Their destination was a house known as Old Woodbury in the parish of Gamlingay, a dozen or so miles to the east and over the county border in Cambridgeshire. Woodbury was a large estate on the north-west edge of the parish, and Old Woodbury had been the original manor house until a larger Georgian-style house known as Woodbury Hall was built in the early nineteenth century on another part of the estate.

Old Woodbury stands in the shelter of the greensand escarpment which runs for forty miles across Bedfordshire to Gamlingay. The house itself was rebuilt around 1837 in the stolid gothic-revival style of the time, complete with tall chimneys, crenellations and a fantasy castle gateway. By the time the Crossleys moved there nearly a century later it had grown into the landscape, half-covered with ivy and surrounded by mature trees and lawns and gravelled paths. The house was set among meadows and farmland and overlooked a small wood. Its seclusion was emphasised by the fact that it was only connected to the outside world by a long drive leading to a gate which opened into Drove Road. My father, who lived in the nearby hamlet of Gamlingay Cinques and was the same age as the Crossleys' son John, recalled dashing with the other children who lived at the Cinques to open the gate when the Crossleys' car was spotted coming down the drive. As it passed, pennies would be tossed out of the window for the children to scramble after.

Eight or nine months after taking up residence at Old Woodbury, in the summer of 1933, Winnie Crossley took that fateful joyride with Cobham's Flying Circus which changed her life for ever. Quite possibly she wanted it to change. Winnie's niece Diana Scott describes her aunt as fun, vivacious, outgoing, a party girl who liked a drink and a cigarette, and who lived life to the full with a smile on her face. Frank she tellingly characterised as very nice, but rather quiet. Given Winnie's adventurous and outgoing personality, perhaps the social merry-go-round she had been on since her marriage to Frank seven years earlier had begun to pall and she was simply bored. Perhaps unconsciously she had been looking for some excitement and a new challenge. Now she had found it.

Chapter Two

Take-off

Winnie probably did not realise it immediately, but flying is an addiction. I speak from personal experience when I say that no matter how much flying one does it is never enough to satisfy the craving. And it is an expensive addiction, as I also know. There's an old saying that if you want to make a small fortune out of aviation it's best to start with a large one. Luckily for her, Winnie had enough money to indulge her new-found obsession.

There were women pilots in 1933, but not many. Pilots needed to hold an Aviator's Certificate, which was issued by the Royal Aero Club after passing the required tests, before they could apply for an 'A' Licence from the Air Ministry. Between 1911 and 1927 a total of just nine certificates were issued to women. By 1933 the number of female pilots had increased to 260, among them Winnie's future colleague Amy Johnson, her future friend Lois Butler and her future boss Pauline Gower.

It took courage and determination for any woman to decide to learn to fly. It wasn't the kind of thing they were supposed to do. For some it was a way of defying convention, an escape from the stifling confines of the traditional female lot of wife and mother; for others it was a challenge and an adventure; and for some the attraction was simply the fun of the thing. Probably Winnie's motives were a combination of all of these. It would be interesting to know what Frank's reaction was when his wife announced she was going to learn to fly. There is a hint in an interview she gave to the *Luton News* in 1939 when she was an established aerobatic pilot ('charmingly feminine in spite of iron-like nerves' gushed 'Madge', the reporter), that Frank didn't altogether approve of her decision: 'Her husband, however, is no flying enthusiast. He didn't even like the idea of his wife learning to fly straight – let alone upside down!'

Unsurprisingly the strong-minded Winnie got her way. She could drive, although she admitted in the same interview that she found driving rather tame after flying: "The sky is a much nicer place than roads," she said, "no restricted areas or Belisha beacons."

She chose to learn to fly rather a long way from home, with the Norfolk and Norwich Aero Club, which had been formed in 1927 at a grass airfield on Mousehold Heath to the north-east of Norwich. At around the time Winnie arrived the airfield became the first Norwich airport.

The Norfolk and Norwich Aero Club advertised that it had three machines available at a cost of £1 17s. 6d. an hour for dual instruction, and £1 10s. 0d. an hour for solo hire. These machines were almost certainly de Havilland Cirrus II Moths, two-seat biplane training aircraft. The weekly aeronautical magazine *Flight* carried news from the nation's flying clubs, and on 30 November 1933 reported that the Norfolk and Norwich was 'pleased to welcome a new member in Mrs. F. Crossley, who has joined to learn to fly', and that she had already been flying under the instruction of Mr. Collier. By the 21 December issue she had completed a cross-country flight to Bedford with an instructor.

Learning the basics of flying isn't inherently difficult. When the student has learned how to take-off, how to climb and descend, how to fly straight and level and how to turn left and right, he or she has the basic manoeuvres. The relatively simple wood-and-canvas biplane trainers of the 1930s with their tailwheels or tail skids were more of a handful on the ground than today's nosewheel types, but otherwise the difficulties facing a student pilot then were much the same as they are now: learning how to navigate, understanding weather, how to cope with emergencies and mastering the different types of landing. Aviation lore has it that a good landing is one you can walk away from; a great landing is one where you can re-use the equipment afterwards.

In the 8 February 1934 issue of *Flight* the Norfolk and Norwich Aero Club reported it was 'pleased to welcome back Mrs. F. Crossley, who has returned to complete her training for a licence. She did a very fine first solo after only 7 hr 40 min dual.'

The first solo, when the instructor gets out of the aircraft and tells the pilot to take off, complete a circuit and land on their own, is an experience he or she will never forget. To have flown a 'very fine' first solo after just seven hours and 40 minutes of instruction ('dual') indicates that she had a lot of natural ability.

But while going solo was an important step in the process of learning to fly, it was not the end of it. There was more dual instruction and other hurdles to overcome before she could gain that precious Aviator's Certificate. Winter days are not often conducive to flying, yet Winnie seems to have completed the latter stages of her training very quickly.

She had to pass an oral technical examination of 60 questions. The flying part of the tests consisted firstly of a climb to at least 2,000 feet, followed by a gliding descent to a landing within 150 yards of a point which had been fixed by the examiner beforehand.

The second part of the test was to fly five horizontal figure-of-eights around two marks 500 yards apart while maintaining a height of 600 feet, the landing to be made within 50 yards of a fixed point. This is more difficult than it sounds. Those five figure-of-eights at 600 feet involved the pilot making continuous steep turns alternately left and right, requiring good control of the aeroplane, as did touching down within 50 yards of the target point.

Winnie successfully completed these tests and was issued with her Aviator's Certificate by the Royal Aero Club on 16 February 1934. When she had three hours' solo flying in her logbook she could apply for her 'A' Licence, the equivalent of today's Private Pilot's Licence. Her Royal Aero Club certificate is actually a small but impressive blue booklet, now in the possession of Diana Scott. It contains, as well as Winnie's photograph, the information that the tests were taken at Norfolk and Norwich Aero Club in a de Havilland Cirrus II Moth.

The Cirrus II Moth was the first truly successful British civilian aircraft. A development of the de Havilland DH 60 Cirrus I Moth, it appeared in 1927 just as the first flying clubs and municipal airports were being established and proved to be exactly what the civil market was looking for. A simple yet elegant biplane, it featured the distinctive de Havilland butterfly-wing shaped fin and tailplanes, and a long exhaust pipe running along the port side just below the two tandem cockpits. When flown solo the pilot sat in the rear cockpit. The Cirrus II Moth appealed to flying clubs because it was deceptively sturdy and could take the punishment meted out by ham-fisted student pilots. It cruised at 85 mph, climbed at 650 feet a minute and had a range of 430 miles.

Winnie needed considerably more experience before she could carry passengers or go on cross-country flights – usually twenty hours solo. She underwent further instruction, practising forced landings and learning how to navigate using a map, a compass and a watch. By early April she was approaching the end of her training.

The *Bedfordshire Times and Independent* picked up the story in its 13 April 1934 edition under the headline *Ambition realized: Mrs. F. Crossley qualifies as a pilot*.

> Mrs. Crossley has taken up flying only recently and gained her "A" licence on 9th March, flying solo after seven and a half

hours' instruction. Up till Friday she had flown eight hours solo, and she was determined to put in a further twelve hours over the week-end so that after passing forced landing tests she would be entitled to take up a passenger. As she had to be back at Woodbury by Wednesday evening she was flying every possible moment and at lunch-time on Tuesday had completed the full twenty hours.

The weather was not good for flying in Norwich on Tuesday, as there was rain most of the morning, together with low clouds. Despite this, Mrs. Crossley got in an hour and a half, although she confessed that it was very bumpy and difficult to land. Wednesday saw the culmination of her efforts, for she completed her forced landing tests and had the satisfaction of taking up as her first passenger her twin sister, Miss Daphne Harrisson, in the afternoon. Thus she realized an ambition that was made possible only by sheer determination under difficult conditions.

Afterwards she flew back to Woodbury. Before leaving, she remarked: "What I want to do is to become a really efficient pilot, so that I can do cross country flights, and later, perhaps, own an aeroplane of my own."

Unless she had managed to borrow an aeroplane or hitched a lift in one, she probably returned to Old Woodbury in one of the Norfolk and Norwich Aero Club aircraft with an instructor, who would have flown it back after she landed. One of the large paddocks at Old Woodbury was suitable as a landing ground and was often used by Winnie and visitors by air in subsequent years. Her achievement was also noted in *Flight* the following week: 'Congratulations to Mrs. F. Crossley . . . on passing her cross-country and forced landing tests and consequently obtaining her passenger-carrying certificate. Mrs. Crossley's first passenger was her sister, Miss D. Harrisson.'

Now she had her 'A' Licence from the Air Ministry it was time for Winnie to decide what she was going to do with it. She was still a member of the Norfolk and Norwich Aero Club, and had joined Marshalls Flying School at Cambridge, which was established in 1930 by Arthur Marshall (later Sir Arthur Marshall). She afterwards joined the Northamptonshire Aero Club at Sywell, the Bedford School of Flying at Barton (where she became a Club Vice-President) and the London Aeroplane Club, based at Heston to the west of London. What these memberships gave her was a choice of aircraft to fly and instructors to fly with, and the opportunity to enter the competitions and to attend the various social events these clubs put on for their members.

During her first year as a qualified pilot, 'practising nearly every day', she said she spent almost 400 hours in the air. That's an extraordinarily high number of hours for a private pilot to fly in a year, more than an hour every day, day in and day out. Most pilots when they are first qualified fly to nearby airfields and get to know their local area before moving on to more challenging flights and to learning new skills. Winnie wasn't content with mere sightseeing. While her husband Frank was engaged in the long summer round of golf and tennis, Winnie was busy learning to fly aerobatics.

Like the majority of private pilots I always liked the blue bit – the sky – to be at the top of the windscreen, and the green bit – the earth – at the bottom. But just as there is a flying bug you can catch, some people go on to catch the aerobatics bug once they have their pilot's licence. Winnie doesn't seem to have wanted to be famous or win races or make record-breaking flights, nor indeed to be the best female aerobatic pilot in the country, which is what she eventually became. She simply seems to have been obsessed with the problem of mastering the difficult art of aerobatics. Being able to fly was something that most people, especially women, couldn't do. Apart from any thrills that throwing an aeroplane around the sky might bring, it may have been part of her motivation that it was something that not many private pilots could do either, which gave it an extra layer of exclusivity.

Flying aerobatics is one of those skills that beyond a certain amount of instruction you have to teach yourself. No doubt it was the need to fly and practise as often as possible that led her, in August 1934, to purchase a five-year-old de Havilland DH 60G Gipsy Moth, registered G-AAET. Winnie based it not at Old Woodbury but at Old Warden, near Biggleswade in Bedfordshire.

Old Warden was the private aerodrome of Richard Shuttleworth, who came from a landowning family which had made its fortune from manufacturing. He had learned to fly in 1932. Shuttleworth was already a successful racing driver whose operation was based at the famous Brooklands track, and he bought a de Havilland DH 60X Moth in order to commute between there and Old Warden. His Moth still flies from Old Warden, and has lived at one aerodrome for longer than any aeroplane in aviation history that's still airworthy.

Exceptionally reliable, the DH 60G Gipsy Moth Winnie purchased was very similar to the Cirrus Moth in which she had learned to fly. It retained the delightful flying characteristics of its predecessor, but had a more powerful 100 hp de Havilland Gipsy engine, and a steerable tail skid which made it much easier to handle on the ground. Francis Chichester (later Sir Francis) flew his DH 60G solo from Croydon to Australia, arriving in January 1930, a few months before Amy Johnson famously made the same journey in another DH 60G.

Winnie was obviously very proud of her aircraft and had some air-to-air photographs taken of herself at the controls of G-AAET. In one she is seen on a sunny winter's day over Old Woodbury, with the low sun casting long shadows across the fields. In another she is flying inverted. Some were taken against a dramatic cloudscape, one of which was used by her to create a personal postcard. Above the caption *Up She Goes* is a three-quarter rear view showing the left-hand side of the Gipsy Moth. Since she's flying solo Winnie occupies the rear seat. She's looking at the camera over her left shoulder, her goggles are pushed up onto her head and she looks as if she's smiling. She probably was, because in the many photographs that were taken of her during her lifetime she nearly always has a smile on her face – and usually a cigarette in her fingers.

A month after buying the aircraft she had gained enough confidence to give what was probably her first public aerobatic display. The occasion was the charity flying display put on by members of the Northamptonshire Aero Club at Marsh Leys Farm, Kempston, near Bedford in September 1934. In its report of the event the *Bedfordshire Times and Independent* stated that Mrs. Crossley, 'who took her flying certificate in record time'

> delighted the crowd with a wonderful spin dive from a height of nearly a thousand feet, and her landing was skilfully accomplished.

Other attractions included flour-bombing a car, rescuing Bedford's beauty queen from 'a gang of roughs', a gliding display, an air race and a demonstration of the Miles Hawk, a racing aircraft flown by the renowned pilot Flight Lieutenant Tommy Rose.

One of the oddities of being a newly-qualified pilot is that simply having a pilot's licence brings automatic acceptance within the world of aviation. If you are a pilot you are on an equal footing with other pilots, no matter what differences may exist between you in background or income or experience. You can fly, and that's all that matters. An attractive, easy-going woman like Winnie would have had no difficulty mixing with a First World War fighter ace like Tommy Rose or any other big 'name' in aviation – and she would eventually come to know most of them.

In December 1934 *Flight* noted that Winnie was taking a course in advanced aerobatics at Sywell. Three months later under the headline *Woman 'Stunt' Flier* the *Biggleswade Chronicle* reported that Winnie was

> one of the first women pilots in England to take up advanced
> aerobatics. She took special tuition in this from Mr. Cecil Bell,
> one of Sir Alan Cobham's pilots. Her stunts include spins, slow
> rolls, flick rolls, the pulling loop and inverted flying.

Newspaper reporters rarely have even a passing understanding of aviation. The manoeuvres Winnie had been taught were not 'stunts', they were the basic elements which, when combined, produce an aerobatic sequence.

Chapter Three

The Art of Aerobatics

It was around this time that Winnie met a serving Royal Air Force (RAF) pilot who would come to play a very important part in her life. In an interview with a Canadian newspaper a dozen years later she said she had met then Flight Lieutenant, later Captain, Peter Fair in 1934 '"in the air" quite literally. She was flying her own Gypsy Moth and Capt Peter Fair . . . came along in another aircraft'.

Peter Fair was a Canadian from a colourful family. His father, William Fair, an insurance agent in Kingston, Ontario, already had six children when he married for a second time around 1901. His bride, Sophia Cleugh (pronounced Clew), was fourteen years his junior, and together they produced a further seven children. Of Sophia's children, Peter's elder brother Howard Fair was an internationally-renowned polo player and horseman who would serve with the Canadian Army during the Second World War, and finish it with the rank of Colonel. Peter's sister Virginia, two years his junior, was a well-known musician and entertainer, broadcasting nightly as the *Songstress of the Peaks* on the Canadian Broadcasting Company network from a hotel in Banff, before going on to have her own show called *Virginia Fair Entertains*.

Peter had three younger brothers: Arnold, who joined the Royal Canadian Mounted Police; Arthur, who became a sergeant-pilot in the Royal Canadian Air Force (RCAF); and the youngest, born Alfred Davidson Colin Cleugh Fair in 1913, of whom more will be said later.

Peter was born in Kingston in 1906, the same year as Winnie was born, and became a cadet at the Royal Military College of Canada (RMC), where he was notable as a sportsman. He spent his summers with the RCAF, and by the time he graduated in 1927 he had already gained his wings. The RMC *Review* of June 1927 said that 'when he graduates he is going into the RAF, where we wish him every success.' The accompanying photograph shows a handsome young man in the uniform of the RMC, though the pill-box hat strapped under his chin and worn on the side of his head makes him look rather like a hotel bellhop.

He duly crossed the Atlantic in 1927 and joined the RAF. By May 1928 he had been promoted to the rank of Flying Officer. He was sent to Malta in 1929 to join No. 446 (Fleet Reconnaissance) Flight, operating six Fairey IIIF aircraft. Powered by a 570 hp Napier Lion engine, these were large, two-seat general purpose biplanes which could lumber along at a top speed of 120 mph In 1931 he was with (No 1) Coast Defence Co-operation/Training Flight at RAF Eastchurch on the Isle of Sheppey in Kent, which also operated the Fairey IIIF. A further promotion to Flight Lieutenant came in 1933, shortly after his unit had been redesignated Coast Defence Training Flight and moved to RAF Gosport near Portsmouth.

In the late 1920s and early 1930s the peacetime RAF resembled an exclusive flying club, and Peter Fair would have found life on an RAF station very congenial. Officers combined rigorous training with ample leisure, which gave them the opportunity to take part in the social scene, sometimes in an official capacity: in March 1931 Flying Officer Fair was among a number of RAF officers presented to King George V at a levee held at St James's Palace. Some of Peter's leisure time was taken up with playing ice hockey. A versatile forward who primarily played on the left wing or in the centre, he turned out for United Services, London Lions and Grosvenor House Canadians. The latter played on a rink situated in the basement of the Grosvenor House Hotel until they became the Wembley Canadians in 1934. A photograph of the Wembley Canadians team in full gear, taken on the ice in 1934, shows the moustached Peter Fair staring seriously at the camera. It was an appropriate look: he took the sport seriously, and was good enough to play regularly for England from 1928. He represented Great Britain at the 1932 European Championships held in Berlin, where he played four games and scored two goals, and at the World Championships in Milan in 1934, making five appearances without scoring.

Like many other RAF officers at the time, Flight Lieutenant Fair also flew for fun. When he first met Winnie it was in the air while she was flying her Gipsy Moth in early 1934, but it's very doubtful if he was flying an RAF aircraft at the time. Whatever the circumstances surrounding that first meeting, the handsome RAF officer and the attractive Winnie Crossley obviously got on well, for in April 1935 *Flight* reported that among the visitors to arrive by air for the Norfolk and Norwich Aero Club's annual dinner were 'Mrs. F. Crossley and Flt. Lt. P. Fair in a Desoutter'.

The Desoutter high-wing monoplane was built in small numbers for use as a trainer, for pleasure flights and as an air taxi. It was the epitome of modern aircraft design, an Art Deco-style angular two-seater featuring an enclosed cockpit, a wide undercarriage and a tall rudder. Richard Shuttleworth bought three of thcm when he set up an air taxi and aircraft hire company called Warden Aviation, which was initially based at Heston before it moved to Old Warden. It was probably one of the Warden Aviation Desoutters that Winnie and Peter Fair took to Norwich in April 1935, perhaps the very one that still lives and displays at Old Warden. Their arrival in it would undoubtedly have attracted attention.

Winnie sold her Gipsy Moth in April 1935, the new owner basing it at Norwich. From now on she would hire the aircraft she flew for fun. It was during 1935 that Winnie's skills as a pilot first began to attract wider attention. In September she gave an aerobatic display at the Norfolk and Norwich Aero Club's annual garden party, came second in the London Aeroplane Club's forced landing competition and won their aerobatic contest. At the opening of Shoreham Airport, *Flight*, whose reporters knew what they talking about, said, 'Mrs. Crossley put up the cleanest aerobatic display we have ever seen by a lady pilot; she was flying a Tiger Moth, and her technique was good enough for the most ambitious male pilot'.

By the chauvinistic standards of the day that was high praise indeed. The following month she entered the Norfolk and Norwich Aero Club's cross-country competition for the President's Trophy. 'This year there were more entrants than usual, and for the first time the trophy was won by a lady pilot – Mrs. F. Crossley, who obtained full marks'.

The *Tatler* photographed her at Heston in full flying suit and sheepskin-lined boots, sitting beside her twin sister Daphne. She appeared in *The Bystander*, again wearing her flying suit, this time captured while shaking hands with the owner of a private airfield at Denham in Buckinghamshire after arriving by air for a tea party. No fewer than 150 pilots flew in to take tea, but it was Winnie's photograph that appeared in the press. She had an indefinable aura about her. She had charisma. She was now a personality in the world of aviation and beyond, one of the best female pilots, and one of the best aerobatic pilots of either sex in the country. But by the time she collected the London Aeroplane Club's aerobatics trophy at a dinner and dance held at the Park Lane Hotel in London just before Christmas 1935, she was no longer the most famous member of the Harrisson family.

* * *

At 1.30 a.m. on Thursday, 28 November 1935 Winnie's father Ernest Harrisson was called to 13 Ferrars Avenue, a council house in Eynesbury on the outskirts of St. Neots. It was the home of Walter and Doris Miles and their two-year-old son Gordon. Mr. Miles was a lorry driver. Mrs. Miles was pregnant, and expecting to give birth to triplets in two months' time. The messenger sent to Dr. Harrisson at The Shrubbery said that Mrs. Miles was losing a lot of water. At just after three in the morning, Dr. Harrisson, assisted by a district nurse and Mrs. Miles' mother, delivered a baby girl, shortly followed by a boy. A few minutes after five o'clock another boy was born. Then, after giving the mother chloroform, an unexpected fourth child, another boy, was delivered and required artificial respiration from the doctor. He weighed in at a little under three pounds. The four babies were placed in two armchairs in the living room and cared for by two district nurses. Dr. Harrisson later wrote: 'It was impossible to maintain an even temperature in the room, which was in a council house, and I therefore decided that the babies would have to be moved, and this was done on November 30th at 6 p.m. We had prepared a room in my home for their reception, and the services of four trained nurses from Great Ormond Street Hospital for Sick Children, London, were obtained'.

To feed them, supplies of breast milk were fetched twice a day by car from a hospital in London. Their father, Walter Miles, 'drives to London and back, a 200-mile trip, daily for this milk', Canadian newspaper *The Streetville Review* told its readers on 12 December 1935, adding that: 'Mrs. J. F. Crossley, daughter of Dr. Harrisson, is a licensed pilot and has volunteered to fly to London for the milk in case any difficulty occurs in making the road trip'.

Other newspapers expanded on the story. It was widely reported that

> Daily air trips to supply the babies with sterilised human milk from London are being contemplated by Mrs. Winifred Crossley, a daughter of Dr. Harrisson.
>
> Mrs. Crossley is an experienced pilot and only recently sold her plane. She intends, however, to hire one especially to fly the milk from Hendon, landing on the Common near St. Neots.

None of the newspapers reported that she actually made a flight and it's unlikely that she ever did. The December weather and the short winter days would make daily flights almost impossible, added to which was the difficulty of landing safely on St. Neots' Common, to say nothing of taking off again. A couple of weeks after the babies were born milk supplies from London were augmented from a hospital in Bedford. The papers did report that an oxygen tent was to be flown by air ambulance from Croydon to Old Warden and that: 'Dr. Harrisson is sending his chauffeur to the aerodrome to take the 'tent' and the man who will demonstrate it to the doctor, to St. Neots'.

Although the oxygen tent arrived safely, in the event it was not required.

The birth of what quickly became known as the St. Neots Quads was an overnight sensation. To give just one example, two days after they were born the *Daily Mirror*'s lead story was *Quads Born in Council House – All Doing Well* which featured a photo of Mr. Miles introducing his son Gordon to 'four future playmates'. Although quadruplets had been born in Britain before, what made Ann, Ernest, Paul and Michael the focus of so much attention was the fact that this was the first time all four babies had survived the birth for more than a day or two. Dr. Harrisson's wife admitted to a reporter that 'we are all frightfully excited' by the quads and said that although she had seen hundreds of babies she had never seen any 'with such beautifully clear pink complexions... they are just perfect', adding 'I do hope they will live'.

She was not alone in that hope. Daily bulletins on their progress were posted on the gates of The Shrubbery, and the daily newspapers carried those updates to their readers. The King sent a cheque for £4. The newsreels were quickly off the mark, as Dr. Harrisson wrote:

> December 24th and 25th were busy days for the nurses and babies, as the Gaumont British Film Company came and took the first films, and on December 25th the mother and father visited the babies for the first time.

It's possible that local knowledge played a part in Gaumont British being allowed to film the babies. Gaumont's publicity manager, Hugh Findlay, lived at Havelock House in Gamlingay. It's more than likely that he knew Winnie Crossley and that she was Dr. Harrisson's daughter. If he did manage to exploit that connection to get permission for Gaumont to take the first footage of the quadruplets who were, as the commentary claimed, 'at the centre of the world's news', it was quite a scoop.

Just four minutes and 38 seconds of that footage shot over Christmas made it to the cinema screen. To modern eyes the whole newsreel is very wooden and carefully staged, accompanied by the relentless cut-glass commentary employed by newsreels at the time. The most natural and charming part is when the stars of the show take centre stage, and the quads are seen with their nurses being fed, weighed, bathed ('not in water but in warm olive oil') and dressed. As the voice-over admits: 'We really are privileged in showing you these pictures because our cameraman saw the babies actually before their mother did... everybody wants to know how the quads are progressing, including their father and mother who paid a call on Dr. Harrisson and his wife.'

The parents were filmed walking up the drive at The Shrubbery, where they were met by Dr. Harrisson and his wife. Extraordinary as it may seem, Mr. and Mrs. Miles had not been allowed to see their children until they were almost a month old.

In the absence of a house big enough for their needs the babies spent their first six months in the nursery at The Shrubbery under the care of Dr. Harrisson. They were famous, and so was Dr. Harrisson. It had taken several years for the press to stop referring to Winnie as Mrs. F. Crossley – an appendage of her husband – and start referring to her as Mrs. Winifred Crossley, but for a long time after the birth of Britain's most famous babies she was invariably described in the press as the daughter of the doctor who delivered the St. Neots Quads.

Chapter Four

Circus Performer

The day after Mr. and Mrs. Miles had been allowed to visit their children *Flight* carried a paragraph stating that a new aviation company would be starting in 1936. It was an announcement that would have great significance for the doctor's daughter.

> Sir Alan Cobham's air circus has been disbanded, but all the equipment has been acquired by C.W.A. Scott's Flying Display Ltd., which has recently been formed. The chairman of the new company will be Mr. C.W.A. Scott, [and] the managing director Capt. P. Phillips . . .

Charles William Anderson Scott was a couple of years older than Winnie, and one of the best-known flyers in the world. After serving in the RAF and working as a commercial pilot in Australia, Scott made his name as a record-breaking aviator. In 1934, flying a specially-designed twin-engine de Havilland DH 88 Comet, he and Tom Campbell Black won the 1934 Mildenhall to Melbourne Air Race, the £10,000 prize and instant worldwide fame. Their Comet now belongs to the Shuttleworth Trust and is still airworthy.

By purchasing Cobham's operation at the end of 1936 Scott intended to use his fame to repeat Cobham's success, but Cobham was a shrewd businessman and Scott was not. Cobham had realised that aviation was no longer a novelty. Partly as a result of his own relentless drive to make Britain air-minded, there were now many permanent airfields and several domestic airlines. The public appetite was moving towards larger air shows, including those put on by the RAF

Scott's new company employed many of Cobham's pilots and staff, including those who brought their own equipment such as Joan Meakin, a skilled glider pilot who flew aerobatics in her German Wolf glider, and Captain Percival Phillips, Scott's business partner in the venture, who used his Avro 504s for joyriding and aerobatic displays. Scott knew he needed to freshen up Cobham's staple diet of barnstorming and joyriding with something novel to draw in the crowds. To that end the company purchased de Havilland DH 82A Tiger Moth G-ADWG, had the fuselage painted in a distinctive red and white chequerboard scheme, adapted the fuel system for inverted flying and employed Winnie Crossley to give aerobatic displays in it. She was familiar with the Tiger Moth, a type which first flew in 1931 and would go on to be built in huge numbers as a trainer. Its great advantage was that it was forgiving and easy to fly, but difficult to fly well: instructors could easily identify unsuitable students, although a Tiger Moth would rarely bite a clumsy one. It was simple to maintain and rugged enough to handle the punishment meted out by both trainee pilots and rough grass fields.

To receive payment for displaying the Tiger Moth Winnie must have had her 'B' Licence, the professional pilot's licence. The requirements were stringent, with various flying tests and examinations to pass including night flying and instrument flying, but if successful the holder of a 'B' Licence was able to fly 'for hire or reward', including carrying passengers. To fly outside United Kingdom airspace (and the tour's itinerary included the Irish Free State) she needed and must have obtained a second-class Navigator's Licence. For international flights beyond 600 miles a first-class Navigator's Licence was required.

The new company's publicity department played up the novelty of a female aerobatic pilot for all it was worth. The press release sent to local newspapers prior to a display to help drum up business promised that: 'Mrs. Crossley, the famous British airwoman, who has achieved the distinction of being the first woman to enter the ranks of aerobatic pilots, will prove that even in this sphere women can hold their own with the men.'

The *Wells Journal* named her their *Woman of the Week*, calling her 'one of Britain's finest airwomen' and going on to say:

> At present she is preparing to tour the country in a large flying circus which will give displays in most of the big towns, Mrs. Crossley giving exhibitions of aerobatics at each performance.
>
> This accomplished airwoman is the daughter of Dr. E. H. Harrisson who attended the St. Neots' quadruplets.

Scott's advertising called Winnie 'The First Woman Aerobatic Pilot', while the show's programme stated that she was 'the first woman to demonstrate aerobatics'. Newspapers dubbed her 'Britain's only woman 'stunt' pilot'. None of these descriptions was strictly true. Doubtless other women pilots looped and rolled and spun aircraft for fun. But Winnie was the first professional female aerobatic pilot in Britain, and probably in the world. Twice a day she would loop and roll and spin that red-and-white chequered Tiger Moth because she was getting paid for doing so.

It was suggested, no doubt for sound advertising reasons, that Winnie found 'a Guinness a day helped her to stand the strain of daily aerobatic flights'. Unfortunately alcohol and aviation do not mix, and not surprisingly the General Manager of the display had banned alcohol. Captain Phillips solved the problem by obtaining a doctor's certificate for her which said she had to have a glass of Guinness each day. In the dotty world of advertising it didn't matter whether Winnie actually drank a daily Guinness or not, so long as the company could claim she did.

The organisational and planning difficulties involved in putting together an air display that would be on tour for six months were enormous. Once the itinerary had been decided upon the venues had to be chosen and checked for suitability. The display was going to use over 150 sites and give two displays at each. Often they were simply meadows. Six weeks or so before the display local newspapers and the local authorities were informed of the date. Three weeks in advance the publicity machine swung into action with a local campaign of advertisements and posters, and in the week leading up to the show, bills were posted around the local area. A limited number of free flights were given to local newspapers for them to give away to their readers.

The convoy of support vehicles carrying the maintenance engineers, ground attendants, catering and laundry staff, along with the tannoy van which carried a large trumpet speaker on its roof, the tanker holding 800 gallons of fuel and the lorries loaded with equipment, all arrived on the morning of the display. Direction signs were put up on trees, telephone poles and lamp posts. Gates were set up, attendants positioned to take the entrance money, and large hessian screens erected around the site to stop spectators who had not paid their shilling admission (children sixpence) from seeing the show. The 'Aero Show Marquee' was put up, containing pictures and models of aeronautical interest and where enamel badges of Scott's famous Comet could be purchased. The banners and flags and the numerous tents for the support personnel to sleep in were also set up. The pilots, who wore white overalls sporting a pair of wings (ground engineers wore black overalls) were accommodated in local hotels. The show opened with a massed flypast of aircraft designed to draw attention to the display about to commence, each one peeling off in turn to fly low and fast along the crowd line before landing.

The first public display took place on 7 April 1936, the Tuesday of Easter week, at the Ace of Spades' airfield at Hook, to the southwest of London. The Ace of Spades was a roadhouse on the Kingston by-pass, one of those curious places which appealed to fun-seeking motorists of the 1930s. Sitting beside a roundabout on the by-pass, it was a combination of filling station, garage, café restaurant and nightclub, which offered dancing every evening and a swimming pool that was open all night. In 1933 the owners acquired a small grass field a few hundred yards away and turned it into an airfield to entice private pilots to visit by air. Little work was needed: like most airfields at the time it had no runways, merely a large white circle painted in the middle of it. Pilots took off and landed directly into wind, as indicated by a windsock. So long as an aircraft passed through the circle it was using the maximum run available.

The publicity department had some photographs taken as the pilots were preparing for their tour, and as it got underway. Winnie was photographed perched on the fuselage of her red and white Tiger Moth, her feet on the pilot's seat, wearing white flying overalls, white helmet and goggles and smiling down at the camera, every inch the glamour girl of the display. In another picture she sits on a rug in front of the diminutive Hillson-Praga Air Baby with her seven-year-old son John, who is wearing a white flying helmet and goggles of his own. Mother and son were also photographed sitting in the cockpit, the blurb claiming 'John accompanies her on all her flights'. The Air Baby was a two-seat, high wing monoplane with an enclosed cockpit, its job to give trial flying lessons on tour. Registered as G-ADXL and painted a vivid yellow all over, the aircraft was actually the second prototype. Advertised as *The Cheapest Light Aeroplane on the British Market!* it cost £385 to buy new, including a 36 hp engine. It was on loan to Scott's tour, but not for long: after a month it left on an epic journey to South Africa.

Winnie was photographed sitting in the cockpit of one of the Avro 640 Cadet three-seaters, a picture notable because it is one of the few ever taken of her not smiling. More publicity shots were taken at the display on 12 April at New Barnet, where Charles Scott himself made an appearance, along with actors Aileen Marson and Billy Milton, who were doubtless hired to bring a little film star glamour to the occasion. They were pictured with Winnie, again resplendent in white overalls and flying helmet, fooling about in and around the display's orange and black Autogiro and watching as Miss Marson raised the Civil Aviation flag to open proceedings.

Flight attended that first display at the Ace of Spades' airfield, and featured a three-page illustrated report in its next issue.

The ground was soggy, the wind cold and gusty, and the aerodrome by no means oversized or level, but apart from a few minor boggings the whole show went commendably smoothly. An encouraging crowd – its ranks were noticeably swelled by local scholars who had just "broken up" that day – lined the enclosure.

Not all the aircraft were available for this display, which opened with the customary mass flypast. Each aeroplane leaving the formation 'dived noisily and, one regrets to record, alarmingly near the crowd'.

Captain Phillips kicked off the entertainment by taking up two passengers in one of his Avro 504s, elderly two-seat biplane trainers which had been adapted for joyriding by the addition of an extra seat. *Flight* reported that Phillips showed the crowd 'just what an ex-Service type trainer will do in the way of aerobatics if asked nicely', dropping a coloured streamer at 1,500 feet and carving it into small ribbons as the Avro spiralled down to land. Cornishman Captain Percival Phillips DFC was a vastly experienced pilot, having learned to fly with the Royal Flying Corps during the First World War. In 1924 he bought an Avro 504 and launched his barnstorming and joyriding career, taking aloft an estimated 91,000 passengers over the next fourteen years. He and Winnie would become firm friends during that summer of 1936.

As pilots H.A. Shotter and L.J. Rimmer began taking up a steady stream of joyriders in another Avro 504 and the Avro 640 Cadet, they were joined by one of the two Airspeed Ferries on the company's books. The ungainly but practical Ferry had two engines on its lower wing and another on the top wing. It could carry ten passengers and had little bother getting in and out of confined spaces, the task for which it had been designed. The six horse-power BAC Drone, a powered glider, was flown back and forth along the enclosure by Idwal Jones, who demonstrated the type's stability by holding both arms in the air and waving at the crowd. Jones, who was known as the 'Wizard of the Air', shared the red and white Tiger Moth with Winnie on the tour, demonstrating inverted flying by circling the airfield upside down, and also using it to flour-bomb the clowns.

Then came the Cierva C30 Autogiro, flown by Ronald Ashley. It was an odd-looking machine, a combination of aeroplane and helicopter with gangly undercarriage, large free-spinning rotor blades to provide lift and an engine for forward motion. Although it could not hover, it could take off and land almost vertically.

Winnie followed, *Flight*'s photographer capturing her with the Autogiro touching down in the background as she taxied out in the Tiger Moth 'to give the visitors their next periodic dose of aerobatics'.

> And a pleasant potion it was, with nice clean loops and rolls and a pukka professional polish. The machine had a fuel system adapted for inverted flying, so Mrs. Crossley took advantage of this for a few seconds.

Captain Phillips in an Avro 504 towed Joan Meakin aloft in her Wolf glider, and after release she brought it looping and stall-turning back to earth. As *Flight* pointed out, the first display was really a dry run for the season to come. One of the Airspeed Ferries, two Cadets and the Hillson-Praga were absent, as was the Flying Flea, a tiny homebuilt aircraft with some fundamental design flaws which eventually saw it banned as too dangerous to fly. Also missing was Idwal Jones' spectacular trick while flying a Cadet of picking up a handkerchief with a wingtip, and his inverted flying display and flour bombing from the Tiger Moth. Martin Hearn's wingwalking act, a parachute descent, an air race and other popular items designed to cater 'for the purely spectacular tastes of the crowd' were also omitted from this first display.

With the addition of the missing acts and aircraft, this was in essence the show that toured the country that summer of 1936: a mix of daring displays and comedy acts to entertain the spectators alongside the joyriding, which was where the real money was to be made.

* * *

After displaying at The Ace of Spades the show moved on to the next venue at Chesham on 9 April, and life on the road began in earnest. No doubt everyone was optimistic that it would be a successful and profitable tour. Over the Easter weekend the display appeared at Dorking and Redhill. At New Barnet on Easter Sunday and Bank Holiday Monday the biting wind with snow and hail 'drove people into the marquees for shelter'. Thetford was next on 16 April, the first of a run of shows at different venues each day lasting until 4 May, taking the operation zigzagging across the south from Bury St Edmunds in Suffolk via Kent and Sussex to Slough and Swindon, then on to the west country including Exeter and Bristol before heading to the midlands. In Bristol Flight Lieutenant Tommy Rose made an appearance, as he was to do on several further occasions during the tour, demonstrating the Miles Falcon and posing for a photograph alongside Winnie and C.W.A. Scott.

Every opportunity was taken to publicise the display. Local garages often displayed the diminutive Flying Flea in their showroom windows. In Rickmansworth Winnie made a personal appearance along with the Flying Flea in the foyer of the Odeon during the showing of a film called *Woman Tamer*.

The 5 May was a spare day, when after a month's hectic work they could finally draw breath. The weather had not been kind, but nonetheless local newspapers were enthusiastic in their reports of the displays. When the tour resumed at Derby on 6 May the weather was not ideal with rain and a gusty wind, and when Idwal Jones was flour-bombing the clowns from the Tiger Moth a wingtip touched the ground and both upper and lower wings were damaged, though Jones was not.

After visiting Llangefni on Anglesey for a display on 8 May they crossed the Irish Sea to appear in Phoenix Park in Dublin two days later. The newsreel cameras were present at Phoenix Park and filmed Captain Phillips performing aerobatics in his Avro 504. The newsreel also shows the flypast, the Autogiro, the Wolf glider and the Flying Flea. Martin Hearn is seen wingwalking, standing on the top wing of Phillips' Avro 504 while holding on to a wire with one hand and waving to the crowd with the other. According to the appreciative report in the *Irish Times* a huge crowd of 40,000 watched the display, although the paper's assessment of Winnie's part in it had distinctly patronising overtones:

> "Aerobatics" by a male pilot have lost their novelty, but when a women performs them she undoubtedly excites the admiration – if not the envy – of the female element in the crowd. Mrs. Winifred Crossley is the first British airwoman to take up "aerobatic" flying, and her performance over the Fifteen Acres was certainly well worth watching. Looping-the-loop, rolls and half-rolls were performed in a manner that made them look easy, and with a "finish" that a male pilot might envy.

Making aerobatics look easy has always been the difficult part.

The Irish leg of the tour lasted almost six weeks, taking in both the Irish Free State and Northern Ireland. With no day off scheduled the itinerary was relentless, although glider girl Joan Meakin did take a snapshot of Winnie and Captain Phillips sitting in a jaunting car during a brief interlude of relaxation. The show visited a new venue every day, taking the display to every corner of

Ireland. Each new landing field provided its own challenges to the pilots: five of them were racecourses, one of them Leopardstown. The display at Waterford's Kilcohen Park racecourse on 28 May was visited by *Entre Nous*, the byline of the anonymous author of a rather camp weekly gossip column in the *Waterford Standard*. After interviewing Joan Meakin he (or she) spoke to Winnie Crossley:

> Another engaging personality whom I had the good fortune to meet on Thursday was Mrs. W. Crossley, a charming brunette, whose frank and amazingly blue eyes twinkled at me over the rim of a glass of limejuice in the lounge of the Adelphi Hotel as she told me her air experiences.
>
> And unusually interesting they were, too. Mrs. Crossley has the distinction of being the first woman to enter the ranks of aerobatic pilots. Her daring display on Thursday left one rather breathless as she looped, rolled and spun to the accompaniment of gasps from the ground spectators.
>
> "When did you first commence flying, Mrs. Crossley?" I asked her.
>
> "Well," she said, as her slim fingers selected a cigarette from my case, "the obsession, it really became an obsession with me, to fly, came rather suddenly. Two years ago I visited an air display, and after that decided to become a pilot. I have never regretted the decision."
>
> "How long were you flying before you became an aerobatic pilot?" I asked.
>
> "Twenty hours," she answered simply.
>
> "Amazing," I could only murmur.
>
> Before her slim figure, clad in white overalls, entered the car Mrs. Crossley told me she was sorry she did not take me up that afternoon.
>
> I murmured, "So was I," but I don't think I meant it. Her 'plane was much too erratic for my peace of mind.

The show packed up and left Ireland on 18 June and pitched up for their next display the day after, at Llanfairfechan on the north coast of Wales, then gave two displays in Birmingham and another at Long Eaton. The scheduled display at Bakewell in Derbyshire on 24 June was cancelled because at the last minute the Air Ministry deemed the field unsuitable for flying.

The north-west was next on the itinerary, which took in Merseyside, Manchester and Blackpool before heading north over the border into Scotland. While in Liverpool Winnie, the 'celebrated woman aviatrix', made a personal appearance in a city store to announce the winners of the 40 free flight tickets given away to the readers of a local paper.

In Scotland the tour kept up its rigorous schedule, performing at a new venue every day for twelve days. It reached its most northerly point when it visited Aberdeen on 8 July, attracting 'large crowds in spite of the unfavourable weather' who saw Winnie's aerobatic display 'which ended with a power dive and a rocket zoom into the air, in a spectacular manner'. They moved down the east coast of Scotland via St Andrews to reach Edinburgh, then crossed to Kilmarnock before entering England once more to display at Bretton Park in Wakefield. Despite the rain and the mud Winnie gave 'a remarkable demonstration. It appeared as simple for her to fly upside down as right way up'.

From Yorkshire the display headed south to Walsingham in Norfolk and then round the coast of East Anglia to end July in Hastings, Sussex, where bad weather led to the show being abandoned. At this stage in the summer, after four months on the road, there are hints that all was not well. Money was always tight, and a wet summer was making matters worse. Prices were reduced in an effort to bring in spectators.

But the show had to go on, and they all headed west into Cornwall and Devon. They displayed at Lynton on the north Devon coast on Thursday 13 August. Next morning the ground crew and all the equipment set off for the two-day display at Weston-super-Mare scheduled to begin later that day. One five-ton lorry, loaded with £2,000-worth of equipment, was being driven by 27-year-old mechanic Lawson Clarke. His mate, Thomas Young, 26, was also in the lorry's cabin. They had set out just after eight o'clock, but while descending the notoriously steep and narrow hill leading into Lynmouth the lorry ran out of control, and approaching a hairpin bend it smashed through a wall, plunged thirty feet into the garden of a house and came to rest upside down in the grounds of a hotel. The driver was killed, but his mate was flung out and although injured he survived. Photographs of the wreckage show what the *North Devon Journal* called 'the shapeless mass of twisted metal and wood work'. Captain Phillips the managing director of the display, visited the site; so did Winnie Crossley. She was photographed standing among the wreckage, watching as workmen rescued what they could of the load of aircraft spares, oil drums and petrol cans. They were transferred to another lorry which took them to Weston-super-Mare in Somerset. However difficult it must have been for all concerned to deal with the death of one of their number in such horrific circumstances, the show still had to go on.

After Weston-super-Mare the display headed north again, performing at Stockport. It reached Clifton near Brighouse in Yorkshire on 23 August and for a change the weather was good. Scott was in attendance and must have been pleased to see the large crowds 'gathered at the hilltop village', brought by special bus services from the local area. The *Halifax Evening Courier* chose to head its report *Clifton Air Display – No Untoward Incidents*, but despite a disappointing lack of newsworthy mishaps the paper observed that 'the planes were taking-off with passengers continuously for five and a half hours'. It was still sunny a few days later at Hull, where they made use of Hedon aerodrome, but the Hillson-Praga Air Baby and the Autogiro were absent being overhauled, and only one of the Airspeed Ferries was available for joyriding.

As September arrived the display should have crossed the Irish Sea once again, with two shows scheduled to take place in Belfast on the first and second of the month, but the weather had other ideas and the first display had to be cancelled. After two weeks of glorious weather, low clouds, rain, mist and fog forced most of the pilots to turn back and wait for conditions to improve. Flying the Autogiro, Ronald Ashley left Blackpool but twice turned back and landed further up the coast. He made it to Belfast at the third attempt, telling a reporter it was one of 'the nastiest flights I have ever made', and that at times he could not see the water, 'although I was flying about six feet above it'. The only other pilot to arrive was Captain Phillips in his Avro 504, who took a huge risk by flying above the clouds and fog. His luck was in when he found a gap in the clouds at his destination. As if bad weather was not enough, the lorry containing the Flying Flea and Joan Meakin's glider was stuck on the quayside at Liverpool because of what were called 'unexpected difficulties' in getting it on board ship.

The others arrived the next day, although 'Mr Scott's daring pilots, including Mrs. Winifred Crossley' had been forced 'to battle with the elements all the way over the Irish sea to reach Belfast' before the tour could get going again. After displaying at Belfast the intrepid aviators moved on to give a show at Bangor the next day. In Ballymena the local paper said of Winnie that: 'She held her audience enthralled with a series of loops, spins, stalls, swoops and rolls, and it was indeed a wonderful moment as the crowd watched her do the "figure [of] eight".'

This second Irish tour was confined to Northern Ireland and ended after performing at ten different venues. By this time it was clear that C. W. A. Scott's Flying Display was rapidly running out of steam. It displayed at Warwick on 18 September, and at Solihull on 19 and 20 September, where Harry Ward, who claimed to be Britain's only 'bird-man' and who seems to have joined the tour towards its end, made an appearance. Wearing a parachute and an outfit with canvas and metal bats' wings attached to it, he made a free-fall descent from 6,000 feet. Unfortunately conditions were unfavourable, and 'his imitation of a bird's flight was not easily visible, and he was not seen until he floated through the clouds, the high wind causing him to land half-a-mile away'.

Tragedy struck again on 19 September, the day of the first display at Solihull. Scott's friend Tom Campbell Black, his co-pilot when they won the Mildenhall to Melbourne Air Race two years earlier, was in a Percival Mew Gull waiting to take off at Liverpool airport when a taxiing RAF Hawker Hart collided with it, its propeller slicing through the cockpit and killing Tom Campbell Black. To make matters worse, that night £150 in cash, the box-office takings for the day's display, were stolen from a company van parked at the Solihull flying field. Perhaps losing his friend and then the day's takings were the final straw for Scott, and he pulled the plug on the tour. So far as can be discovered the second display at Solihull on 20 September seems to have been the final display by the last big flying circus ever to tour the United Kingdom.

The display was dogged by bad luck and a wet summer. That it was wet, cold and miserable most of the time is confirmed by Pauline Gower (of whom more later), who toured the country in 1936 giving joyrides with the smaller British Empire Air Display. In her book *Women With Wings* she called the weather that summer 'uniformly bad throughout', and her chapter on the 1936 season is full of comments about how terrible the conditions were. For Scott's larger display with its bigger overheads this meant that money was always short, but the difficulties were compounded by the problem that fundamentally it was simply one tour too many. The novelty of flying had worn off. More than five months after their first display at the Ace of Spades, the men and women of C.W.A. Scott's Flying Display, who had led a nomadic existence roaming the country and entertaining the crowds, went their separate ways.

At the start of the tour it had been claimed the display would visit more than 150 sites throughout the United Kingdom. The venues where displays are known to have taken place adds up to 117, but only eight are known for August 1936, and just 14 for September, though it's more than likely that other shows were given before the tour finished on 20 September.

Three days later a receiver was appointed, and at the end of October C.W.A. Scott's Flying Display Ltd was put into voluntary liquidation, the company saying in a statement that

> the unfortunate trading results were due almost entirely to the abnormally bad weather experienced during the summer of 1936.
>
> On a number of days the complete flying programme had to be cancelled owing to adverse climatic conditions, so that it can be seen that this company had an unfortunate summer for its inception.

The company's assets were sold. Winnie's red-and-white chequered Tiger Moth was purchased by the Cinque Ports Flying Club at Lympne, Kent and repainted in the Club's blue and silver scheme.

Chapter Five

The Show Goes On

In 1935 Captain Phillips had set up a company called Air Publicity Ltd, based just to the west of London, at Heston. Now the 1936 display season had ended he turned his attention to exploring ways of using aircraft as an advertising tool. His fleet consisted of eight Avro 504Ns, a Simmons Spartan II three-seater and the two Airspeed Ferries that had toured with C.W.A. Scott's Flying Display.

Air Publicity's main business was banner-towing, for which the Avro 504N was ideal. It was powered by a 180 hp Armstrong Siddeley Lynx radial engine and featured a modified undercarriage with the forward skid of the earlier 504s removed. Air Publicity further modified their aircraft: a box containing a quick-release gear was added under the rear fuselage, and the rear cockpit decking was cut down to accommodate three passengers when used for joyriding.

The company manufactured its own banners on-site at Heston. The letters (five feet high) were made of strengthened black canvas and could be hooked together to form the message, which could have between 15 and 30 letters and measured from 150 to 250 feet long. The tow line which attached it to the aeroplane was 400 feet long.

To get a banner into the air it was first laid out on the airfield in the form of a letter 'J', the banner forming the long downstroke and the rope and the aircraft making the curve. A steel tube was used as a stabiliser fin between the tow rope and the first letter. An engineer held the steel tube at about shoulder height. As the Avro took off the pilot would wait until he or she could feel a pull on the tow-rope, then lower the nose and peel the banner off the ground. When the towing aircraft was ready to land it first flew low over the airfield and released the banner. As with the flying circuses, if an airfield was not available the company would make use of a suitable field.

By now highly-experienced, Winnie Crossley joined Air Publicity as a contract pilot, paid by the hour. She was the only female pilot on the staff and considered herself to be very well paid for the work. Her first banner-towing assignment was over Luton. The company had contracts covering much of the country, which meant the aircraft were often away on tour for a fortnight and more.

While on tour the pilot flew with a licensed engineer. The Avro's rear cockpit would be loaded with everything needed to operate away from Heston, such as ten-gallon oil drums, tools, spares and luggage, plus the engineer. A driver-mechanic followed them around in a van carrying spares and a sewing machine for repairing the letters.

The reason the venerable Avros were considered to be the most suitable aircraft for banner-towing was because they were powerful enough to get airborne quickly and possessed a good rate of climb, yet had the ability to fly slowly so the banner could be seen by the maximum number of people on the ground. Banners were towed at around 50 mph, and on one occasion when flying into a strong headwind over Glasgow, Winnie found herself flying backwards over Sauchiehall Street, much to the amusement of Captain Phillips when she told him.

The changeable British climate often caused problems for Air Publicity's pilots. Just before Christmas 1937 Winnie took off from Walsall Aerodrome to fly a banner over Wolverhampton. While she was away, as a local paper noted, 'the fog thickened, and she could not get back to the aerodrome, so landed on the new aerodrome at Wolverhampton'. This must have been RAF Cosford, officially opened in 1938, one of the many new aerodromes springing up all over the country as the Royal Air Force rapidly expanded in response to the increasing threat of war.

Air Publicity was very successful. Clients were charged £20 for a two-hour display, which could potentially be seen by a million people or more. Its aircraft toured the coastline of Britain in summer carrying banners such as *Corona – Britain's Better Beverage* and *Bile Beans Nightly Keeps You Fit*, and flew over huge sporting events such as the Derby, the Grand National, the FA Cup Final and the Boat Race. The British public were exhorted to listen to *Radio Luxembourg 6.30 Tonight*, or to *Drink Ovaltine For All Day Energy* or to *Join The Auxiliary Fire Service*. The Government were the target of one banner that Winnie flew over Whitehall in July 1937, which read *Give All Civil Servants Pensions*.

Captain Phillips found the flying rather dull after his barnstorming days, describing his job as one of the most boring in aviation. He found some satisfaction in towing gliders for the London Gliding Club on Dunstable Downs, an activity in which Winnie joined him. The qualities that made the Avro 504N so suitable for towing banners made it equally capable for towing gliders. Winnie found that in an hour she could tow seven gliders in succession to 2,000 feet, using around a gallon of fuel on each tow.

The enlarged rear cockpit of the Avro was also suitable for mounting cameras to take air-to-air footage for films, and Air Publicity's 504s were used on George Formby's *It's in the Air* (1938), on *Lightning Conductor* (1938) starring Gordon Harker, and on *Q-Planes* (1939) with Laurence Olivier and Ralph Richardson. Impossible to tell now, but Winnie may have done some of the flying involved.

So far as is known Winnie was the first woman to tow banners, and the first to tow gliders. But old habits die hard and Winnie also kept her hand in with her first love. On Coronation Day 1937, flying a hired Tiger Moth, the *Biggleswade Chronicle* reported that she

> offered to fly over to Bedford and provide a thrill for the youngsters on their afternoon. The large concourse of people assembled in Mill Meadows witnessed a splendid programme of aerobatics. The exhibition included slow rolls, half rolls, loops and rolls from the top of loops as well as stall turns and spins. The weather at the time was not too good, and unfortunately there was no sun to shine on the beautiful machine or its daring pilot.

As 1937 drew to a close Winnie could reflect on her two successful years as a commercial pilot. Although we'll never know for sure, it seems probable that by then she had come to the conclusion that her 11-year marriage to Frank was also coming to an end.

* * *

In 1935 Flight Lieutenant Peter Fair was posted to Iraq, though not to a squadron. Instead he joined the RAF's No. 1 Armoured Car Company, based at RAF Hinaidi, near Baghdad. The unit consisted of 18 armoured vehicles, and because there were no British troops stationed in Iraq its job was to provide support for the RAF squadrons that were based there.

In Iraq he made the acquaintance of Vivien Grafftey-Smith, the wife of the British Consul in Mosul, a city in the north of Iraq. Her husband, Laurence Grafftey-Smith, said he noticed a change in his wife's attitude towards him during 1935, stating that Flight Lieutenant Peter Fair was 'associating' with his wife at the time. She promised not to see him again. Later, Grafftey-Smith discovered some love letters, concluded that she had committed adultery with the Flight Lieutenant and sued for divorce. The *Daily Mirror* said the adultery had taken place 'at a camp in Iraq' when reporting the uncontested Divorce Court proceedings in October 1937. The judge granted a decree *nisi*, gave the custody of the children to the husband and the bill for costs to Peter Fair.

Six months before the divorce hearing, Peter Fair had left the RAF at his own request after serving for ten years. He became an airline pilot, probably with Imperial Airways Ltd, and then later with British Airways Ltd. When he was mentioned in the papers again he was described as 'a commercial air pilot'. He was in the news because of a shocking event that occurred at Gamlingay on Sunday, 13 February 1938.

Winnie's friend and employer, Captain Percival Phillips, had been banner-towing in Avro 504N G-ACRE over Hull and Grimsby that morning. The previous day the east of England had been battered by northerly gales of 80 mph, and while the wind had abated a little it was still blowing very strongly. While returning to Heston Phillips decided to land at Old Woodbury and visit the Crossleys. One account has him arriving to find the Crossleys were not there, and guessing where they would be, taking off again and buzzing the White Horse Inn at Eaton Socon, on the Great North Road near St. Neots. He then followed Winnie in her car back to Old Woodbury, his wingtip 'close to the car window all the way', Phillips hedge-hopping as necessary. Given the gale force wind blowing, the story seems highly unlikely.

The escapade, if it really happened, was not mentioned later in court. Rather it heard that Captain Phillips, who had flown into Old Woodbury before, arrived from Hull at about 1.15 p.m. and had lunch with Winnie, her husband Frank and Peter Fair. It has since been speculated that Winnie had decided to leave Frank and marry Peter Fair, but while that is a possible reason for Fair's presence at Old Woodbury, there is no knowing whether it was to discuss matters with Frank or not. The suggestion is that Phillips was upset by the prospect of Winnie and Frank separating, and that it contributed to what happened next. It's a doubtful conclusion given Phillips' vast flying experience. What is known is that Phil, as Winnie called him, took off at 3.15 p.m. from a field below the house to return to Heston. Frank Crossley, Peter Fair and presumably Winnie were watching. The take-off was into the very strong and blustery northerly wind.

Peter Fair was an experienced pilot, and he said in evidence that the Avro climbed to about 200 feet then made a left-hand turn and came back across the field. The aircraft had lost height in turning but the engine was running perfectly. To the horror of the onlookers the 'excessively strong wind' carried the Avro helplessly into a 70-foot high tree. The impact caused the machine to crash nose-first to the ground, where the wreckage began to smoke.

Frank Crossley said he 'and others' ran to get the pilot out. One of the others was Peter Fair. The two men managed to get the unconscious Captain Phillips clear of the wrecked aeroplane just before it went up in flames. They both received burns. The Captain's dog, Kim, securely wrapped in a blanket in the rear cockpit, was rescued unharmed. By the time Gamlingay's policeman arrived on the scene at 4.10 p.m. the pilot had been taken into the house and was 'being attended by Dr. Harrisson of St. Neots'. Doubtless he had been summoned by his daughter. From there the badly-injured Phillips was transferred to Bedford Hospital, arriving at 5.15 p.m. He had multiple injuries and a fractured skull. He never regained consciousness and died half an hour after admission.

My father, who was nine years old at the time, remembered the crash happening and said the police wouldn't allow anyone to visit the site until a week or so later, after the wreckage had been cleared away. Someone, however, managed to take a photograph of the skeletal remains of G-ACRE. It appeared a few days later in the *Cambridge Independent Press*, showing the field where it lay now covered in snow and the fateful tree with its branches broken in the background. Most of the front end of the aeroplane has burned away, but the metal framework of the fuselage is intact.

Winnie said it was her 'most awful day', and that 'Phil had been such a chum'. At the inquest the Coroner praised the courage of Frank Crossley and Peter Fair in extricating the pilot; each man had a bandaged hand from the burns they received. The Coroner expressed sympathy with Mrs. Phillips in her sudden and unexpected loss and the jury returned a verdict of accidental death. Mrs. Phillips was left to bring up her two sons on her own.

Flight's short obituary said the Captain was 'a particularly charming and modest man, with an almost boyish zest for flying'. Another noted that 'he was never happier than when he was in the air, and that fear or 'nerves' were entirely unknown to him'.

Despite the death of Captain Phillips, Air Publicity Ltd continued trading. As always in aviation, the show goes on. *Sailplane and Glider*'s obituary said that he was to have done most of the towing at the forthcoming Leicester meeting, 'but his place will now be taken by Mrs. Crossley'. The meeting took place over Easter 1938 and the dozen or so gliders were towed by Winnie and released at 2,000 feet.

On 23 June 1938 Winnie was on a banner-towing assignment that took her and her flight engineer Bernard Downs from Heston to Birmingham. In the afternoon they left Birmingham to fly to Yeadon, now known as Leeds–Bradford Airport, when the weather closed in. 'Raven-haired, smiling Mrs. Crossley' told the *Yorkshire Observer* what had happened:

> "We hit clouds and mist over Derbyshire and Sheffield, and finally, although I was only six miles from Yeadon, I decided I must come down.
>
> "I circled round, and selected this field in preference to another which I could see had not been mown."

The field was in Bierley, a suburb of Bradford. Winnie's matter-of-fact account of her sensible precautionary landing was given added drama by the newspaper:

> Watched by hundreds of people, she circled the suburb flying low over the houses on the new estate in search of a suitable landing ground.
>
> She flew so low over the links of the West Bowling Golf Club that players ran for safety.
>
> Eventually, the pilot selected a field that had been newly mown, and completed a perfect landing on the fringe of tall grass and near a group of horses.
>
> Several hundred people had been attracted to the scene by the sight of the low-flying machine. It appeared so low sometimes, indeed, that householders feared it would hit the chimneys.
>
> The silver-grey Avro 'plane was undamaged. As soon as it landed people rushed forward and helped to move it under the shelter of a wall.
>
> The pilot and her engineer were invited by nearby residents in Broughton Avenue to stay at their houses until this morning, when they will probably take off again to complete the flight . . .

Three weeks later Winnie left Heston to do some glider-towing at Dunstable. With her was Captain Phillips' spaniel Kim, making its first flight since it had survived the fatal crash at Old Woodbury. Kim 'seemed to relish the flight, looking over the side down at the people who watched the 'plane land'. Winnie spent the week towing gliders from the nearby private airfield at Studham belonging to Alan Butler, a wealthy businessman who had learned to fly in 1921. That same year he ordered a private aeroplane to his own specification from de Havilland, liked the company, invested in it and became its chairman in 1923, a role he held until he retired in 1970. He married Lois Reid in 1925. She too became infected with the flying bug, and learned to fly in 1929. Alan and Lois Butler became Winnie's lifelong friends.

With war looking increasingly likely, Romford Flying Club set up the National Women's Air Reserve. Within two months more than 200 women had been recruited.

> Further evidence that women are more than holding their own in aviation was supplied at Romford Airport, Harold Park, on Saturday when women pilots Mrs. Winifred Crossley and Pauline Gower performed flying feats, which, according to the amplified commentary, "would be beyond the capacity of the ordinary male pilot."

The commentary was given by Dorothy Spicer, Pauline Gower's business partner, a pilot in her own right and the first woman to earn all four Air Ministry engineer's licences. She described the opening event

> in which Mrs. Winifred Crossley, the famous aerobatic pilot, and Miss Pauline Gower, who has carried more than 27,000 passengers – a world's record for a woman – took part [including] missing the wind indicator by a margin of feet, and high-speed dives which flattened out a few yards above the grass.
>
> Miss Gower and Mrs. Crossley also took part in a short closed circuit three-lap race round the aerodrome. Miss Gower led for the first lap, but Mrs. Crossley took the lead in the second lap and held it until the end.

The type of aeroplane Winnie flew on this occasion was not mentioned in the report. The odds are it was a Tiger Moth, for as the Munich crisis was coming to the boil in September 1938 Winnie gave an impromptu 'but nevertheless polished' aerobatic display in one at Cardiff airport, while a large crowd waited for the competitors in the London to Swansea air race to pass overhead. A little over a month later she performed at the Civic Air Day at Norwich, again in a Tiger Moth.

A precautionary landing like the one she carried out near Bradford is made when the pilot decides it is safer to be on the ground than in the air. A forced landing is when the pilot has no alternative but to land, usually because of engine failure. Winnie had two engine failures while flying the old Avros. One was over Dumfries, where she managed to land safely in a field and local Boy Scouts guarded the aeroplane over the weekend. The other, rather more alarmingly, occurred while she was towing a banner over 100,000 people gathered at Wembley Stadium for the 1939 F.A. Cup final. The headlines in the papers the next day varied: one screamed *PLANE NEARLY FELL INTO CUP FINAL* while another contented itself with the more restrained *Trouble Over Cup Final – Woman Pilot's Coolness*. This time Winnie had to drop the banner and make a hurried forced landing on a golf course at Sudbury, half a mile or so from Wembley Stadium. According to the *Biggleswade Chronicle*'s account

> . . . she said 'Sorry, chaps,' to the golfers whose game she disturbed and offered them cigarettes.
>
> 'I was making my way with difficulty back to Heston when I had to come down,' she told a reporter.
>
> 'I was afraid that the golfers would be annoyed with me for spoiling their game, but they were charming.'

By then it was clear that war with Germany was coming. Frank Crossley gave in his notice at Old Woodbury in May and was commissioned in the Royal Artillery in June. It was probably at this period that an anonymous head-and-shoulders portrait of Winnie in profile was painted. She's wearing her white flying suit, white flying helmet with pink goggles and a pale cream scarf patterned with small black dots. Her head is tilted up slightly and she's looking at the sky. It's beautifully done in Art Deco style and looks rather romantic, its elongated format suggesting it might have been intended to be used on a cigarette card.

Most of the banners Winnie towed now were aimed at recruiting people for the armed services. There was time for one last aerobatic display, at Redhill on 29 July. *Flight*'s report called it

> smoothly conventional, with a final spin from which recovery was made in 'only just' measure. With a Tiger Moth the recovery height was safe enough, and the autorotation was slowed carefully down with increasing opposite rudder so that the dive-out was completed accurately and at low altitude alongside the enclosures.

A month later all civilian flying ceased, and on 3 September 1939, war was declared on Germany. The golden age of flying was over.

Chapter Six

Anything To Anywhere

In 1938 Captain Peter Fair won an award 'for maintaining an efficient service between Croydon and Paris'. Afterwards he was flying on the Berlin, Warsaw and Stockholm routes for British Airways Ltd., but once war was declared those routes were suspended, for obvious reasons. On 21 December 1939 he was the commander of a Lockheed 14 Super Electra registered G-AFYU on a scheduled flight from Alexandria in Egypt to Croydon Airport. There were eleven people on board: five crew and six passengers. The Super Electra was a tubby, all-metal twin-engine American aircraft with an H-tail, which cruised at around 200 mph. British Airways had a fleet of eight of them, and they represented a great leap forward in speed, comfort and reliability.

The aircraft made a scheduled stop at Sollum, a coastal airfield 300 miles from Alexandria on the far north-western corner of Egypt. From there it took off at 8.55 a.m. heading across 730 miles of the Mediterranean to Malta. It made a routine radio call to Malta at 10.20 a.m., and then – nothing. Five hours later with the aircraft overdue, efforts were made to contact it but proved fruitless. No distress call had been received. A search and rescue mission was launched, with British and Italian ships and Italian aircraft taking part (Italy did not declare war on Great Britain and France until June 1940). However, it was a French ship, the *St Georges*, which rescued the survivors from the sea near Sicily and landed them at Malta.

Why the Super Electra came down is not known: presumably the details were kept quiet because of the war. Only six men survived the ditching in the Mediterranean. Three of them were passengers: an RAF Wing Commander, a Lieutenant in the Royal Navy and an Army Major. Three of the crew also survived: the Flight Engineer, the Steward and the Captain, Peter Fair, who suffered a broken arm. Three other passengers and two members of the crew died.

The newspapers reported the search for the lost airliner and those on board, and then the welcome news that six survivors had been found. Winnie must have been frantic with worry until she learned that Peter was safe.

At the same time as the press was reporting the story, it was also printing news that eight leading female pilots had been recruited to join a new Women's Section of the Air Transport Auxiliary (ATA) to ferry 'the light type of trainer aircraft from factory to aerodrome'. The *Daily Mirror* of 23 December 1939 even carried the two stories next to each other on the same page under the headlines *Ace Women Pilots* and *British Air Liner Missing*.

* * *

One of the ace women pilots was Winnie Crossley. On her ATA application form dated 1 December 1939, she gave her address as Newhaven Court Hotel in Cromer, Norfolk, and her normal peace-time occupation as 'Air Publicity'. She had flown a total of 1,860 hours, of which five had been at night (the ATA stipulated that women should have at least 500 hours in their logbooks, twice that required of men). She said she had flown most single-engine aircraft, had a 'slight knowledge' of twins, had owned her own Gypsy Moth and had flown in both the British Isles and in France.

The Air Transport Auxiliary was the brainchild of Gerard d'Erlanger, a merchant banker and private pilot who was also a director of British Airways. He had realised that the coming war would see a shortage of pilots. In August 1939 he put forward his idea that a pool of civilian pilots not eligible for the services because of age or health should be gathered to fly light aircraft with the aim of transporting mail, dispatches, medical supplies and ambulance cases. Thirty male pilots were selected. It very quickly became clear that the real need was for pilots to ferry aircraft from factory or storage to the operational squadrons, and that became the ATA's job for the duration of the war and beyond. Its pilots joked that the initials ATA stood for Anything To Anywhere.

Pauline Gower, the daughter of an MP, who had been a barnstormer since 1931 and was a highly-experienced pilot, pushed for and was given the job of recruiting eight women pilots to ferry Tiger Moths from the de Havilland factory at Hatfield to wherever they had to go. She was appointed the Commander of this new Women's Section. A dozen women were selected to undergo flight tests on 16 December 1939 at Whitchurch airfield, Bristol. The tests were undertaken in a Tiger Moth by A.R.O. Macmillan, a British Airways instructor who had been recruited to test ATA applicants.

When the tests were over, eight of the women were selected, all of them qualified flying instructors. Winnie, with hundreds of hours in

Tiger Moths, was one of them. She had been a qualified flying instructor for at least a year and probably much longer than that. The others chosen were Margaret Cunnison, the first woman in Scotland to become a flying instructor; Margaret Fairweather, daughter of Lord Runciman; international ice-hockey player Mona Friedlander; diminutive 21-year-old Joan Hughes who had got her 'A' licence aged 17; Gabrielle Patterson, the first British woman flying instructor; Conservative MP's daughter Rosemary Rees, and Marion Wilberforce, the daughter of a Scottish laird. Aviation was (and is) a small world and many of them knew each other from pre-war days.

The ATA was entirely separate from the RAF, a purely civilian operation which at various times came under different organisations, but which was administered throughout its existence by d'Erlanger and his staff. The First Eight women, as they have since become known, were paraded before the press at de Havilland's Hatfield aerodrome on 10 January 1940, a cold and sunny day during a bitter winter. There was a touch of frost on the grass. Photographers like to have the light behind them when taking their photographs; consequently in nearly all the resulting pictures the women are squinting into the dazzling rays of a low sun, with the photographer's own shadows intruding in the foreground. Parked de Havilland Tiger Moths can be seen in the background of many of the photographs.

The Women's Section had its own uniform which had to be worn on leave and in London: a dark blue jacket bearing the ATA wings, a forage cap, dark blue skirt and black stockings, along with a greatcoat to keep out the cold when necessary. In the air the women could wear dark blue slacks or cumbersome Sidcot suits depending on the weather.

The photographers insisted that the women, already wearing their new Sidcot suits, flying helmets with goggles and fur-lined flying boots, should pick up their parachutes and run to the Tiger Moths as if they were fighter pilots scrambling to intercept a German raid. They duly picked up their parachutes and scrambled, and did it again and again until the assembled photographers were satisfied. For some unfathomable reason petite Joan Hughes was photographed balanced on top of a step-ladder and even Pauline Gower had to sit in the cockpit of a Tiger Moth, smiling and waving a gloved hand vaguely in the air. Then they went inside and pretended to be studying maps or helping each other out of the Sidcot suits. Finally they changed into their dress uniforms, went back outside and posed in them as well. Winnie told a reporter somewhat disingenuously: "My husband is out in France, so I have closed down our home until the war is finished. He is in the Army, not the RAF. He prefers to leave flying to me."

Newspapers and magazines up and down the country lapped it up, with headlines like *Air Girls Go Into 'Action'* and *Women Pilots Aid The RAF*. The *Daily Mirror* excelled itself by printing a picture of one of the women seen from the rear, clad in her Sidcot suit, boots, helmet and parachute and headlined 'How D'ye Like the Togs, Girls?', with the caption

> Perhaps it doesn't look quite so chic as your usual confections, this Air Transport Auxiliary uniform.
>
> But we LIKE you in your harness, and the bustle which is a parachute. We like your air; in fact, we LIKE you flighty!

There's nothing like treating the introduction of the first women to be allowed to fly RAF aeroplanes seriously, and this was nothing like treating it seriously. There was already opposition from many quarters to the news that women would be flying RAF aeroplanes, and this kind of frivolous coverage only made matters worse. Ironically, in his 'Cassandra' column in the next day's *Daily Mirror* the writer William Connor (later Sir William Connor) was apoplectic.

> You have recently been subjected to a lot of cissy nonsense about gorgeous air girls flying scrumptious aeroplanes for the ducky-wucky women's section of the Air Transport Auxiliary.
>
> These beautiful bird girls (complete with fearless dancing eyes) amount to just one great bubbling heap of guff.
>
> They look well enough prinking themselves up in their cockpits, but in point of fact, they are mincing around monopolising planes that could be used for getting on with the serious job of winning the war . . .
>
> But these little girls, who look so well in the pictures, might as well be told that when the real stuff starts they'll be no damn good flipping hither and thither burning up good petrol and ferrying loads of damn all there and back again . . .
>
> Flying chorus girls are grand for peacetime.
>
> But they are just a yapping wasteful headache when there's a war on.

The Hatfield photocall created a lot of publicity, and was the beginning of the press's enduring fascination with the women of the ATA. Throughout the ATA's existence there were many more male pilots than female ones – seven times as many – but the public had gained the unfortunate impression that it was an all-women organisation.

This is probably as good a moment as any to get something straight: the women of the ATA did not go into 'action'. They were not, as the *Daily Mail* claimed not so long ago, *The Female Top Guns of World War II*, neither were they *the female air force who once ruled our skies* as the blurb on one recent book claimed, never mind *the women who dared to fly*, as the subtitle to the same book described them. This is to fundamentally misunderstand and undervalue what the male and female pilots of the ATA achieved. Their job was to ferry, not to fight. Their aircraft were unarmed, and they flew them, often having never flown that type before, without radios and with no navigational aids. Pilots navigated visually, using a combination of the quarter-inch Ordnance Survey maps of England and Scotland over-printed in red with the position of airfields, a compass and a stopwatch. They flew by day in all weathers, and weather has always been one of the main causes of flying accidents. Winnie herself said after the war that most of the ATA casualties were due to bad weather. Low clouds, mist, fog, rain, snow, poor visibility and strong winds are common in Britain. It's sobering to remember that during the Second World War more than 8,000 aircrew died in training and non-operational accidents, many caused by bad weather.

ATA pilots made the ultimate decision about whether to fly or not, but were frequently under intense pressure to push on to get a vital delivery completed. They were not supposed to take-off unless the cloudbase was at least 800 feet and the horizontal visibility better than 2,000 yards, or just over a mile. They were supposed to fly below 2,000 feet for recognition purposes and in sight of the ground. They had no training in flying on instruments, and were banned from flying above cloud. It's relatively easy to climb through cloud, but it's a different matter when the hoped-for hole to let down through doesn't appear and you have to descend through the cloud, not knowing what lies beneath. Add in the risk of mechanical failure, the dangers of wartime Britain with its swathes of barrage balloons and nervous anti-aircraft gunners as well as the possibility of running into a German intruder, and it's clear the ATA had a difficult and demanding job.

From February 1940 it took over the ferrying task completely, releasing fully-trained service pilots for combat duties. Figures differ, but some

1,250 pilots from 25 nations around the world eventually served in the ATA during the war, 168 of them women. Fifteen women – almost one in ten – and 158 men were killed. When the ATA was at its peak, Commodore Gerard d'Erlanger told a visiting group from the Army Recognition school that 'Every machine you see in the sky has been, or will be, flown at some period of its life by a pilot of the ATA'. For six years non-stop the ATA pilots delivered the aircraft that British forces needed to fight the war, totalling at the end a whopping 309,000 aeroplanes in all. That was their achievement. No hyperbole is required.

But in January 1940 all that was in the future. After the excitement of the press day, the women began the job of ferrying Tiger Moths from the all-women ferry pool at Hatfield to training bases and storage facilities throughout the country. They knew they were being carefully watched to see how they performed, and that one blunder or one accident would confirm the suspicions of the RAF top brass that women should not be flying their aircraft.

Thus began the next phase of Winnie Crossley's life. In the absence of her logbooks her ATA career has to be uncovered from the official ATA records, in the logbooks of other pilots, and in the books some of them later wrote. Rather than a continuous narrative, we have to be content with occasional sightings of Winnie.

January 1940 was the coldest month since the previous century, and ferrying open-cockpit Tiger Moths was freezing and physically demanding work. (I can testify that a Tiger's cockpit is a cold place to be at 2,000 feet even at the height of summer.) Flights had to stick to recognised routes and be undertaken in gaggles so they could be easily identified by the Observer Corps. Within a month or two the First Eight were joined by a handful of other women, including Winnie's friend Lois Butler. More recruits soon followed, one of them being Amy Johnson. She had learned to fly in 1929 and made her name in 1930 as the first woman to fly solo from England to Australia. Overnight it made her one of the most famous female pilots in the world. Johnson, who had hoped to be given the job of Commander of the Women's Section herself, joined it in late May 1940 after swallowing her pride and taking the flying test. The notoriously icy and intolerant Lettice Curtis, an Oxford triple-blue with a degree in Mathematics, joined a month later. Even she melted a little in the warmth of Winnie's personality.

During the time Winnie was based at Hatfield she rented a large, rambling Tudor manor house in North Mymms called Abdale House, where she put up some of the other women pilots. With eight bedrooms there was plenty of space for them. The house was situated in its own grounds a mile or two south of the de Havilland airfield at Hatfield where they worked.

Although the ATA was not a part of the RAF it had a similar system of ranks. At the end of June 1940 Winnie was promoted to First Officer, equivalent to a Flight Lieutenant in the RAF As the country waited for the Luftwaffe's inevitable assault after the evacuation of Dunkirk, much of the production of Tiger Moths had already been moved from Hatfield to the Morris Motors' factory at Cowley, near Oxford. A pilot tasked with taking a Tiger Moth from Cowley to, say, Hawarden airfield near Chester, needed a lift in an aerial taxi from Hatfield to Cowley, and if possible to be collected by taxi from Hawarden and returned for the next delivery. If no taxi aircraft were available pilots had to get back as best they could, often by train.

For taxi work at this time the women had the use of a twin-engine Avro Anson trainer loaned by ATA headquarters at White Waltham, and what was termed 'Moth variants' like the de Havilland DH 83 Fox Moth and DH 80A Puss Moth. The Anson could carry nine pilots and more plus their parachutes, and featured a manually-retracted undercarriage which required 150 turns of an awkwardly-placed crank handle. The Puss Moth was a high-wing biplane with an enclosed cabin, and room for a pilot and two passengers, while the Fox Moth was basically a Tiger Moth with three passengers seated in an enclosed cabin in front of the pilot, who sat high up in an open cockpit. As well as Moths, Winnie also flew the Miles Magister, a tandem open cockpit monoplane trainer.

Such were the demands of war that by the early summer of 1940 it had been decided that women should fly all types of training aircraft. At some point in that pivotal summer Winnie attended the Central Flying School at RAF Upavon to learn how to fly more complex aeroplanes including twins, which were fitted with constant speed propellers and retractable undercarriages. She flew the single-engine Miles Master advanced trainer and the twin-engine Airspeed Oxford, the latter used extensively by the ATA as a taxi aeroplane. Back at Hatfield she converted to the twin-engine Avro Anson and the de Havilland DH 89A Rapide, a reliable biplane twin that could carry up to ten passengers. There was also a version of the Rapide built as a trainer for the RAF and called the Dominie. Because the two aircraft were much the same the ATA record of Winnie's flying lumps Rapides and Dominies together. She also converted on to the American

Fairchild Argus, a high-wing single-engine taxi aeroplane that could carry three passengers.

Winnie was to spend a lot of her time in the ATA flying taxi aeroplanes, criss-crossing the country delivering and collecting pilots. On the face of it this might seem a rather menial task, but it was in fact a huge compliment to her flying ability. Only the safest and most reliable pilots flew taxis. The calculation was simple, though somewhat cold-blooded. If a pilot ferrying an aircraft crashed and was killed, then it was unfortunate to lose an aeroplane and a pilot, but it would be very much worse if a taxi aeroplane crashed and a dozen valuable pilots died. In May 1941 Winnie's personal record confirmed she was 'an exceptionally good pilot', and that she was 'at her steadiest when acting as a Taxi pilot'.

Philippa Bennett joined the ATA in the summer of 1940. Her logbooks are now kept in the ATA Museum at Maidenhead. A woman after my own heart, she recorded all her passenger flying as well as her own flying as pilot in command, and through them we catch glimpses of Winnie going about her business. On 6 July she flew Bennett and probably a couple of other pilots from Hatfield to Cowley in Fox Moth X2866, and on 1 August 1940, as the Battle of Britain was beginning to hot up, she again took Bennett in a Fox Moth, this time X2865, on a 15-minute hop from Hatfield to Hendon. Lettice Curtis wrote that because the women were only flying trainers the Battle of Britain had little impact on them, and when bombs were dropped near airfields they were visiting or enemy aircraft were shot down, it 'merely added to the day's interest'.

The Battle, which the RAF won by not losing, was effectively over by October 1940, but attacks still continued. On 3 October Hatfield itself was bombed, when a Junkers Ju 88 appeared out of low cloud over the aerodrome and dropped its bombs. One landed close to the ATA women running from their office to the shelter but fortunately didn't explode. Four bombs hit a factory workshop, killing 21 people and injuring around 70 more. The pilot of the Junkers had machine-gunned those dashing for the shelters but his aircraft was hit by the airfield defences and crashed a few miles away. The crew were captured by local farmworkers.

In November 1940 Philippa Bennett records being a passenger in a DH 89A Rapide piloted by Winnie from Hatfield to Wroughton, an airfield near Swindon. The last we see of Winnie in 1940 is in the logbook of Marion Wilberforce, one of the First Eight. On 20 December Winnie took her up as a passenger in a Tiger Moth from Hatfield for half an hour's flying in the local area. This may well have been a routine check flight with Winnie acting as the instructor.

* * *

The new year opened with snow, and it snowed on and off until early March. On 2 January 1941 Winnie, Joan Hughes and Lettice Curtis were flown in the taxi Rapide down to the Miles factory at Woodley, near Reading, to pick up some Miles Masters and ferry them to Ternhill in Shropshire. They had to wait while the aircraft were readied, and this and some local snowstorms delayed them until a break in the weather allowed them to depart at half-past two, well into the short January afternoon. They were flying separately but each encountered snow over the Cotswolds. Flying in snow is a disorientating experience, with visibility next to zero and thousands of snowflakes zipping past the cockpit like tracer bullets. Sensibly they each turned back, Lettice Curtis to land at Little Rissington in Gloucestershire, and Winnie Crossley and Joan Hughes both making it to Upper Heyford in Oxfordshire. The snow next day prevented any flying, but the following morning it had let up and the three managed to reach Ternhill at last, where their Masters were to replace the North American Harvards used by the RAF Flying School there. The three women joined five other pilots who had been flown up from Hatfield, and they took the redundant Harvards to Odiham in Hampshire, where they were crated up to be sent to a training school in South Africa.

At the same time as the women were ferrying the Harvards, Amy Johnson was heading for Prestwick in Scotland, to collect an Airspeed Oxford and deliver it to Kidlington (now known as London Oxford Airport). The weather was poor and after leaving Prestwick Johnson landed at Squires Gate airfield, Blackpool, where she stayed overnight. The conditions were better the next morning, Sunday 5 January 1941, but cloud blanketed most of southern England. After waiting for conditions to improve Johnson finally lost patience and took off just before noon.

What happened during that flight will never be known for certain. It's likely that Johnson was flying 'on top' – above the cloud – but as the hours droned by she had no real idea where she was. She had no radio to ask for assistance and no convenient hole appeared in the undercast for her to drop through and find out. Probably she nosed down into the cloud a couple of times to try and get through, but failed. When, after three-and-a-half hours the engines began to splutter as the fuel ran out, Johnson must have trimmed the aircraft in a glide above the cloud. Then she made her way to the door, wrenched it open and plunged into space. Her parachute opened safely and she floated down through the misty murk. She emerged beneath the cloud over the Thames Estuary off Herne Bay, followed by the Oxford, which glided down into the water and broke up. Seconds later Amy Johnson hit the cold water.

She had been spotted by a convoy not far away. HMS *Haslemere* got to within twenty yards of her, but the heavy sea swept her under the bow of the ship and into the propellers. The captain of the ship jumped in to try and rescue her, but Johnson was never seen again. Overcome by the icy cold the captain had to be rescued by the ship's lifeboat. He died later in hospital.

As Winnie knew from bitter experience, despite the sadness felt by everyone in the Hatfield Ferry Pool at Amy Johnson's death, the show had to go on. In the days that followed there was little flying because of the bad weather. Lettice Curtis wrote that on 9 January 1941, just four days after Johnson died:

> a group of us went to Abdale, the house rented by Winnie Crossley one of our senior pilots. After the inevitable walk we had tea and afterwards adjourned to The Comet where for some reason Winnie, who must have been celebrating something, regaled us with champagne.

The Comet hotel stood next to Hatfield airfield, and was a familiar sight to drivers on the Great North Road (A1) for decades after the war. Winnie was actually celebrating her 35th birthday. How typical of her to order champagne and make a party of it. It may also have been her way of marking the passing of Johnson.

Either way she normally didn't need much of an excuse to party. Veronica Innes (later Veronica Volkersz) joined the Women's Section as a pilot in March 1941 and wrote that Winnie was 'dark and attractive . . . gay and very party-minded'. Alison King, the Operations Officer of the Ferry Pool at Hatfield, said she was 'as dashing and warm-hearted and gay as one could have wished'. Winnie was older and more experienced as a pilot than most of the new recruits. In the air she took the oft-repeated ATA instruction that 'You are paid to be safe, not brave' seriously, to the extent that one of her Commanding Officers later said of her, while acknowledging her to be a 'smooth and polished pilot' and that she 'is at all times an amiable person of great charm and is extremely kind-hearted', that nevertheless he considered her to be 'apprehensive of poor weather to an extraordinary degree for such an experienced and good pilot. Discipline is fair and her influence, which is considerable is not perhaps always in the best interests of the unit.'

There is another way of looking at this criticism. She was apprehensive of poor weather precisely because she was such a good and experienced pilot: she had learned not to take liberties with it. People who did take risks with the weather, as Amy Johnson had done, sooner or later came to grief. Margie Fairweather's husband Douglas was an ATA Anson taxi pilot and renowned as the best bad-weather flyer in the organisation, but even he made one flight too many into poor weather, crashing into the Irish Sea while flying in cloud in April 1944. The adage that *it is better to be down here wishing you were up there, than up there wishing you were down here* was as true then as when it was passed on to me forty years later.

The comment about discipline was echoed in Winnie's final ATA report, written in February 1945, which marked her discipline as average and her leadership as 'Not markedly good', adding that she is a 'pleasant and amiable person who is friendly and helpful to her less experienced colleagues.' All the evidence suggests that in the air she was a very fine pilot, cool, professional and highly-skilled, but that on the ground she enjoyed having fun, and acted as a kind of naughty older sister to the younger women pilots in the ATA. Many of the women who were given the senior jobs in the organisation tended to be ones who would have been bossy head girls at their private schools, and that wasn't Winnie at all. She would have been the one organising the midnight parties in the dorm.

* * *

As the winter turned to spring life continued much as before for Winnie and the other women pilots. Between February and July 1941 Philippa Bennett recorded making thirteen flights in taxi Rapides and Ansons piloted by Winnie, the shortest a ten-minute hop from Hatfield to Luton, the longest an hour and ten minutes from Hawarden near Chester to Hatfield.

But beneath the surface that spring a seismic change was about to happen to the Women's Section of the ATA. There was still a government ruling that women should not fly operational types, but now they were told they could fly 'obsolete' types. One of the obsolete types that Winnie flew was the Airspeed Courier, a five or six-seat light transport of which only 16 were ever built. There was the Westland Lysander, a high-wing aircraft with remarkable short take-off and landing abilities which was being withdrawn from frontline use in early 1941. It later found fame with the Special Operations Executive flying agents into and out of small fields in Occupied France on clandestine night operations. Another obsolete aircraft she flew was the Hawker Hart, a big, powerful and sleek two-seat pre-war biplane bomber which also served under different guises as a fighter and a trainer. She also flew (briefly) the Fairey Battle, a three-seat single-engine light bomber, which was hopelessly outclassed by the start of the war.

On 10 May 1941 the newly-appointed Minister of Aircraft Production, J.T.C. Moore-Brabazon, visited the Women's Section at Hatfield. He was a pioneer aviator who made the first flight in England by an Englishman in 1909, and in 1910 became the first person to qualify as a pilot in the United Kingdom, when he was awarded the Royal Aero Club Aviator's Certificate number one. At Hatfield thirty years later he was photographed in the middle of a bevy of lady pilots, arm-in-arm with Lois Butler and Pauline Gower. A beaming Winnie stands to Gower's left, a pair of white leather gloves dangling from her hand.

Moore-Brabazon had lunch with Gower, Butler and Winnie. It was too good an opportunity to miss and the women pressed the case for being allowed to fly a wider range of aircraft than they were currently doing. Lettice Curtis wrote that Winnie 'was particularly anxious to get her hands on Hurricanes and Spitfires, and the new Minister left with no doubts about the desire – or the ability – of women to play a full part as ferry pilots'.

A little later d'Erlanger is said to have remarked to Pauline Gower, 'I suppose there isn't really any reason why women shouldn't fly Hurricanes'. Gower pounced: 'Fine – when can we start?' The date turned out to be 19 July 1941.

On that pivotal day ATA test pilot Captain R.H. Henderson brought a Hawker Hurricane over from White Waltham to Hatfield. Whenever a pilot transitioned to a single seat aircraft the first flight was necessarily also a first solo. That was not too much of a problem while the women were flying relatively simple types, but the Hawker Hurricane was of a different order of magnitude. It was less than a year since Hurricanes had borne the brunt of the Battle of Britain. The first RAF fighter to exceed 300 mph, the rugged Hurricane far outnumbered its graceful, glamorous stablemate the Spitfire during the Battle, and was responsible for shooting down around four-fifths of the enemy aircraft destroyed. By 1941 it was becoming outclassed as a fighter, but the addition of bombs, cannon and rockets would see it remain in frontline service throughout the war.

Significantly, First Officer Winifred Crossley, with over 2,000 hours to her name, was chosen to make the first flight ever by a woman in an operational RAF fighter. She was the most experienced and the most able pilot, and she held the fate of the Women's Section of the ATA in her hands. It was the chance to prove themselves that the women had longed for, and everyone came out to see Winnie make that first flight. Perhaps she was also chosen because she had been watched by spectators hundreds of times before and was unlikely to be put off by their presence.

She climbed into the cockpit and strapped herself in. Captain Henderson would have leaned in and pointed out where the various controls were situated and briefed her on the starting procedure and the speeds to use. Then it was down to Winnie. She started the 1,030 hp Rolls-Royce Merlin, completed the numerous checks, released the brakes and taxied to the take-off point. After going through the pre-flight vital actions she lined up into wind. Take-off was accomplished by opening the throttle, bringing the tail up as the speed increased and at 90 mph the aircraft was lifted into the air, while keeping the nose down to let the speed build up. 'It was literally with bated breath that we watched Winnie make the first Hurricane take-off', wrote Hatfield's Operations Officer Alison King, one of the onlookers.

As the Hurricane climbed the spectators saw the undercarriage raised. Still climbing, the aircraft turned ninety degrees crosswind before levelling off at 800 feet and 120 mph. After turning another ninety degrees downwind to run parallel to the runway, Winnie would have done her pre-landing checks and lowered the undercarriage. Perhaps she glanced down at the knot of people watching her while she waited until she judged it was time to turn again. The Hurricane was usually landed off a curved approach at about 100 mph A third of the way round the turn the flaps were lowered, with the aircraft still turning until it was lined up on final approach. Crossing the threshold at 85 mph a slight check on the stick brought the nose up a little, then the throttle was cut and the aircraft touched down for an oh-so-satisfying three-point landing. Touching down on the mainwheels and the tailwheel at the same moment was the best way to maintain control on the ground, and it was so satisfying because it was difficult to achieve.

Veronica Volkersz witnessed the event and later wrote that Winnie 'as always did a perfect take-off and landing' adding that she 'watched enviously, wishing I were a First Officer'. Alison King said:

Above: The Harrisson children in 1906. The eldest, Jack, is in the centre, with Winnie on the left and her twin sister Daphne on the right. They were later joined by two more siblings: George in 1909 and Muriel in 1912. Probably taken in the garden of The Priory, then the Harrisson's family home in St. Neots, Huntingdonshire.

Right: Their father Dr. E.H. Harrisson, Christmas 1903. Thirty-two years later this provincial doctor shot to worldwide fame as the man who delivered the St. Neots Quads. Although quadruplets had been born in Britain before, this was the first time all four babies had survived for more than a few days. They generated enormous publicity at the time. Winnie was making her name as a female aviator, but for several years afterwards she was invariably described as the daughter of the man who delivered the St. Neots Quads.

Above: Old Woodbury, Gamlingay, Cambridgeshire. The Crossleys moved here towards the end of 1932. The house had been built a century before in the gloriously silly gothic-revival style which was then fashionable.

Left: This photograph of four ladies following a fox hunt appeared in *The Sketch*, 30 November 1927. It was captioned '*The Pytchley Meet at Cottesbrooke: Miss L. Robinson, Mrs Frank Crossley, Miss Orlebar and Miss Robinson on the coign of vantage*'.

Above: Winnie with her son John.

Below: The postcard she had printed of her flying the de Havilland DH 60G Gipsy Moth G-AAET she bought in 1934.

Above: Winnie's Royal Aero Club Aviator's Certificate, issued on 16 February 1934. She re-signed it 'Winifred Fair' after her marriage to Peter Fair in 1943.

Below: Winnie flying her Gipsy Moth G-AAET against a threatening skyscape.

Above: Winnie flying the Gipsy Moth over her Old Woodbury home. The bare trees and the low sun suggest this was taken during the winter of 1934/35.

Below: The Gipsy Moth inverted. It's probable that these images and those on the previous pages were all taken on the same sortie.

Above: This photograph was probably taken in 1935, maybe at Heston. Left to right: Daphne Harrisson; unknown; Winnie; unknown. Standing in the doorway to the right is New Zealander A. E. Clouston, a well-known record-breaking flyer, test pilot and (later) a senior RAF officer.

Below: Dr. Myles Bickerton and his wife greeting Winnie at an 'air tea party' they hosted at their Denham airfield in May 1935.

Above: C.W.A. Scott's Flying Display had some publicity shots taken before the 1936 tour began. A similar one to this, of Winnie and her son John sitting in front of Hillson-Praga Air Baby G-ADXL, was often used in the tour's pre-show local advertising. Taken 7 April 1936.

Below: C.W.A. Scott, left, with Winnie in her white flying suit, and actor Billy Milton. Actress Aileen Marson is sitting in the cockpit of the Cierva C30 Autogiro. Taken 12 April 1936.

Above: (Left to right) C. W. A. Scott, actors Aileen Marson and Billy Milton, and Winnie, with a very large loudspeaker behind them. Taken 12 April 1936.

Below: Winnie in the cockpit of an Avro 640 Cadet. On the ground she was vivacious and fun. In the air she was a serious professional. Taken 7 April 1936.

Above: Winnie performed her aerobatic displays in G-ADWG, a red-and-white chequered de Havilland DH 82A Tiger Moth. After the tour the aircraft was sold to the Cinque Ports Flying Club at Lympne in Kent.

Below: Tiger Moth G-ADWG is just visible on the left of this photograph. The attention of the spectators is on the Cierva C30 Autogyro flown by Ronald Ashley. Although it could not hover it could take off and land almost vertically. Taken 12 April 1936.

A flypast opened each show during the 1936 tour, taken 12 April 1936. On the far left is Winnie's Tiger Moth G-ADWG. On the right is Avro 504N G-ACRE.

The more usual eight-ship flypast, photographed later in the tour.

Avro 504N G-ACRE flown by Capt. Percival Phillips on the 1936 tour for joyriding and which also carried Martin Hearne while he performed his wing-walking act. Phillips died when the aircraft crashed at Winnie's Old Woodbury home in February 1938.

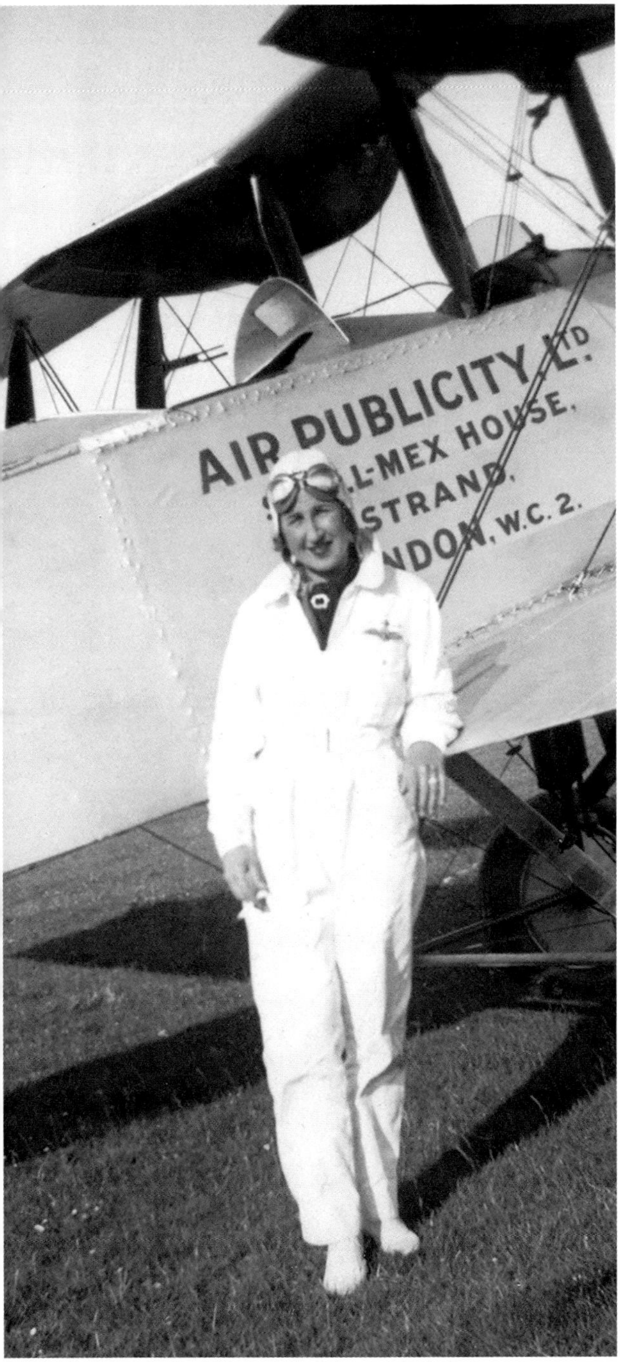

This is to certify that
_________________ has flown
with me and supported
British Aviation. A. Phillips
PILOT.

CAPT. P. PHILLIPS. D.F.C.

Above: Publicity postcard
printed for Captain
Percival Phillips. This one
is not personalised but is
postmarked 1934.

Below: A beaming Winnie
photographed before the
outbreak of war.

Above: Winnie with an Air Publicity Avro 504N,
used by the company for tugging gliders and
banner towing. She has a cigarette in her fingers.
As was common at the time, pilots were often
photographed smoking near aircraft. For obvious
reasons the practice is not allowed today.

Above: Six of the First Eight women to join the ATA photographed at Hatfield on 10 January 1940. Left to right: Marion Wilberforce, Margaret Cunnison, Margaret Fairweather, Rosemary Rees, Winnie Crossley, Gabrielle Patterson. Missing from the photograph are Mona Friedlander and Joan Hughes.

Below: Pauline Gower at the piano in a newly-opened club for service women in March 1940, with Winnie looking on.

Above left: A delightful and sensitive portrait of Winnie by society artist Olive Snell, 1943.

Above right: Winnie and her mother at a christening in 1942.

Below: Winnie's twin sister Daphne's wedding in 1945. John Crossley, Winnie's son, is back left, and her second husband Peter Fair is back, right. In front of them, left to right: Jack Harrisson, Winnie, her younger brother George Harrisson and his wife Ilse.

Examples of some of the many different aircraft types Winnie flew with the ATA.

Top: Hawker Hurricane.

Above: Supermarine Spitfire.

Left: De Havilland DH 89 Dragon Rapide.

Below: Consolidated Liberator.

Above left: Winnie with her close friend Lois Butler at Hatfield. In contrast to Winnie, Lois Butler rarely smiled when being photographed.

Above right: Winnie in the Bahamas in the late 1950s.

Below: This is G–ADEV, one of the Avro 504Ns owned by Air Publicity in the 1930s. Winnie would have flown it many times during her three years with the company. It was rebuilt for the 1950 RAF Display as an Avro 504K and starred in the film *Reach For The Sky*. This venerable aircraft still flies today with the Shuttleworth Collection at Old Warden Aerodrome in Bedfordshire.

Above left: Relaxing with her dogs in the garden of her home in Berkhamsted, Hertfordshire.

Above right: Fooling around on a beach in the Bahamas sometime between 1956 and 1961, when Peter Fair was General Manager of Bahamas Airways.

Below: The Harrisson siblings together for one last hurrah. From left to right, Muriel Cleugh-Fair, Dr. Jack Harrisson, Winnie Fair, Daphne Jessop and George Harrisson.

we watched Winnie make the first Hurricane take-off, do a quick circuit and come in to a perfect three-point landing. As she stepped out and came up to the little group who were to follow her she was her usual debonair self. 'It's lovely, darlings,' she smiled, 'a beautiful little aeroplane.'

The others who followed her that red-letter day were Margie Fairweather, Joan Hughes, Rosemary Rees and Margot Gore. Alison King caught the mood afterwards when she wrote: 'The strain must have been great on these pilots and afterwards there was much laughter and celebration and we eyed each other with furtive, unspoken delight – for we knew that that afternoon something momentous had happened.'

It was the perfect excuse for a party, and they had one in London that evening.

* * *

In the two months after that first flight Winnie spent most of her time flying the aerial taxi service in Rapides, Ansons and the Fairchild Argus as usual. Philippa Bennett records another five trips being taxied around by her at this time. Winnie also managed to put in two hours and thirty minutes on Spitfires. Whether she was ferrying clapped-out aircraft destined for the scrapyard or pristine machines straight from the factory isn't recorded. The Supermarine Spitfire is adored by the public today for its beauty and its iconic status, but almost everyone who actually flew a Spitfire fell in love with it because of its qualities as a flying machine. Not as simple and straightforward as the Hurricane, the Spitfire was a pure thoroughbred, fast, responsive, and manoeuvrable, a true pilot's aeroplane, although its narrow-track undercarriage made it trickier to land and to taxi than a Hurricane.

After that first take-off, circuit and landing in a Hurricane – which probably took 15 minutes at most – Winnie logged more time ferrying Hurricanes. ATA pilot Ann Welch wrote about taking a Hurricane to Scotland in the autumn of 1941 but because of the weather she had to stop and stay overnight at RAF Silloth on the Cumberland coast with other ATA pilots making the same journey. Waiting for the rain to stop the next day,

During the afternoon a few more aeroplanes came in from the sunnier south. Winnie Crossley and Lois Butler landed from

Hatfield in a Dominie to collect Hurricanes for squadrons in Kent, and gave me the latest gossip, then soon afterwards the daily batch of new Hurricanes arrived, and by four o'clock there were fourteen of us waiting for the weather further north to clear.

Lois and Winnie were probably back at Hatfield when it did. The press was still very interested in the Women's Section, especially if any of them were married and had children. Alison King claimed one paper published an article under the title *Mother Knits While Waiting For Her Bomber* while another appeared under the headline *Flying Grandmothers*. King recounts a conversation on the subject between Winnie Crossley (a mother) and Lois Butler (a grandmother):

"Heavens," said Winnie, "must I always have my motherhood thrust at me?"

"A fig for motherhood," groaned Lois, "it's grandmotherhood I want to forget. How did they ever get to know? I don't look like one, do I?" she asked plaintively.

"Of course not, darling," soothed someone. "Not a day out of place, I promise!"

More publicity came when the Ministry of Information's Crown Film Unit made a 30-minute documentary called *Ferry Pilot* on the work of the ATA, which briefly featured an anonymous Ferry Pool 'staffed entirely by women pilots'. Filmed at Hatfield, the women are seen walking towards a taxi Rapide led by Winnie and Pauline Gower. As the pilots clamber aboard, Winnie and Pauline study a map spread out on the Rapide's lower port wing. The film then cuts to a close-up of the cockpit with Winnie taxiing the aircraft past the camera, carefully looking over her left shoulder to make sure she's clear of it.

By the time *Ferry Pilot* was released at the end of 1941 much had changed at Hatfield. Many of the more experienced women had transferred to the all-female pool at Hamble. Joan Hughes and Margaret Cunnison of the First Eight remained at Hatfield and were doing a lot of instructing. In August Winnie was promoted to Junior Captain. Pauline Gower moved to White Waltham, and her place as Commanding Officer at Hatfield was taken by Marion Wilberforce, with Winnie Crossley as her second in command. In October 1941 the new CO's logbook records a 40-minute flight with her second in command in a Puss Moth, from Hatfield up the Great North Road to Sandy and back. This might be a check flight but it looks suspiciously like a jolly.

Less amusing was the incident which took place at RAF Colerne in Wiltshire on 18 November 1941 when Winnie taxied Avro Anson N5060 into an unmarked hole, resulting in damage to the undercarriage. No blame was attached to her, and such incidents were common. Most pilots had to cope with engine failures and forced landings sooner or later. Winnie herself had experienced them during her pre-war commercial flying, and was to have two further and more serious incidents during her ATA career.

Flying a Dominie on 5 April 1942 near Chipping Warden in Northamptonshire, the battery (situated in the baggage hold) exploded and she carried out a successful forced landing. The report concluded she was not responsible. A similar verdict followed another successful forced landing on 9 October 1942, this time in a Fairchild Argus at RAF Waterbeach near Cambridge: 'Following partial engine failure, the aircraft was landed without damage on an aerodrome.'

In February 1942 Winnie was promoted to Flight Captain, the ATA equivalent of an RAF Squadron Leader. A month later she went to the Advanced Flying Training School for Class 4 training. The ATA divided the different types of aircraft they flew into six classes. Winnie was already qualified to fly aircraft in the first three classes – trainers, single-engine fighters and light twins. Class 4 aircraft were twin-engine operational aeroplanes, mostly medium bombers.

Winnie did her conversion course on the Bristol Blenheim, which took her a total of four hours and forty-five minutes, divided between dual instruction and solo flying. With her new rating she could now fly any of the types within that class. The first two Class 4 types she ferried were the Handley Page Hampden and the Vickers Wellington, although she had never flown either of them before. The job of an RAF pilot was to know everything there was to know about one particular type of aircraft and to fly it to its limits, but the job of an ATA pilot was to know just enough about lots of different types in order to ferry them safely. The secret that made it possible to fly an aircraft that was entirely new to the pilot was simple: a dark blue ring-binder with *Ferry Pilot's Notes* printed in gold on the cover, small enough to carry in a uniform pocket. Within the binder were cards containing all the essential information a ferry pilot needed, even if they had never set eyes on the type before. To take just one example, the card for the Bristol Blenheim gave all the necessary technical details to fly Marks I, IV and V, including the stall speeds, how to operate the undercarriage and flaps, and the speed to use on final approach depending on the all-up weight.

On 5 May 1942 Marion Wilberforce noted on Winnie's official record that she was a 'very good pilot and in many ways a valuable Flight Captain'. Which might imply that in other ways, she wasn't. By then Number 5 Ferry Pool had moved from Hatfield to Luton. Wilberforce soon recommended Winnie for refresher training and to undertake the Class 4+ conversion course onto more difficult twins. The refresher part of the course seems to have been flown on Harvards and Blenheims, and the conversion part on a Lockheed Hudson. The Hudson was Lockheed's military version of the Super Electra, the type ditched by Captain Peter Fair in December 1939.

Winnie returned to Luton on 23 June, and in the busy month that followed she flew 133 hours, comprising probably 200 separate flights, or roughly six or seven flights every day. Most of it was taxi work, but she also put in eight hours on Lysanders, spent 12 hours ferrying Hurricanes, an hour and a half in Spitfires, almost 11 hours ferrying Wellington bombers, and an hour and forty minutes flying the Lockheed Ventura, a beefed-up version of the Hudson. She spent 35 minutes flying a geriatric Armstrong Whitworth Whitley twin-engine bomber, and probably most excitingly of all, four hours and ten minutes in the Bristol Beaufighter, a pugnacious and heavily-armed twin-engine fighter which served in numerous frontline roles throughout the war. (The RAF only retired its last Beaufighter in 1960.)

This kind of flying is hard, tiring, concentrated work and it took its toll. Winnie was off work for a fortnight in September 1942, ill with gastroenteritis, and before she could resume flying had to complete a Class 4+ check to make sure she was up to speed again.

Over the winter of 1942/43 she added more new types to her logbook, flying the Douglas Boston bomber, North American's iconic Mustang long-range fighter and the less-successful and largely forgotten British Westland Whirlwind, a twin-engine fighter dogged by unreliable engines. Winnie also flew the magnificent de Havilland DH 98 Mosquito. Her first flight in one probably took place in the late summer of 1942. Captain Geoffrey Wikner, an Australian, described taking off in an Anson one day to deliver nine pilots to three or four airfields. 'Attractive Winifred Crossley happened to have a chit to collect a Mosquito from de Havilland's and it was a "first" for her. To any pilot, and especially a female, it could be somewhat frightening.'

Powered by two Rolls-Royce Merlin engines and with a structure mainly made of plywood, the Mosquito had an outstanding performance. Very fast and capable of fulfilling many roles it served as a fighter, fighter-bomber, night fighter and photo-reconnaissance aircraft. The Mosquito's Achille's heel was its high stalling speed, which meant that after take-off it had a fairly high critical speed of 200 mph, the minimum speed necessary to maintain control should an engine fail on take-off. Mosquitoes were not easy to land either, requiring an approach speed of 125 mph. Wikner continued: 'It was my responsibility to see the pilot safely strapped into the cockpit and go through all the controls, gauges etc. with them. I watched her [Winnie] make a good take off and delivered the other pilots to their pick-up aerodromes.'

Winnie's maiden Mosquito flight was from Hatfield to RAF Honeybourne, in Worcestershire. Wikner's job was to collect the five male and four female ferry pilots from their destination airfields and return them to Luton. 'My last pick-up was at Honeybourne, where Winifred had delivered her Mosquito; she arrived safely and made a good landing.'

Wikner had been delayed several times and it was late by the time he arrived at Honeybourne. The Anson needed refuelling, and as no fuel was available and they were running out of daylight, Wikner suggested they should all stay overnight in the local village. Lois Butler was among the group of stranded pilots and fortunately she knew the owner of a nearby hotel, who agreed to put them up for the night.

> We arrived at the hotel and entered the lounge with its large welcoming fire. The owner and his wife were extremely hospitable, we ordered some bubbly and other drinks.
>
> It was a night to be remembered. It finished with all the girls being put into a large rocking cradle used by a baby King of the past. I shared a double room with a first officer and Winifred and Lois shared another double room. I think the other two girls shared a bed out on the verandah and where the other chaps slept, I hadn't a clue.

Winnie spent no less than fifty-two hours ferrying the Mosquito during the winter of 1942/43. It was an outstanding aeroplane and it's difficult to imagine Winnie not enjoying flying it.

She would not have enjoyed what the new Officer Commanding of Number 5 Ferry Pool, Commander Hills, wrote about her in her personal record in January 1943, assuming she saw it: 'A most capable & 'above average' pilot. Should cultivate a greater sense of responsibility with regard to her duties as Flight Captain, & so justify her rank.'

In May 1943 she was posted to Number 9 Ferry Pool at Aston Down, a mixed male and female Pool high up on the Cotswolds. She would spend the next year there. *Brief Glory*, written by E.C. Cheesman, was published in 1946 and told the story of the Air Transport Auxiliary. Cheesman described Aston Down as 'a sort of wartime country flying club', and gives us this cameo of Winnie there:

> Winifred Crossley, one of the eight original women pilots, is stationed here, and her silver and gold Victorian match boxes, collected from all parts of the country, and converted into lighters, will be shown by their proud owners long after the little Ferry Pool is forgotten.

She quickly added the twin-engine Armstrong Whitworth Albemarle and the Hawker Typhoon fighter-bomber, with its mighty 2,180 hp Napier Sabre engine, to the types of aircraft she had ferried. Then a month after arriving at Aston Down she was sent to the Advanced Flying Training School at Marston Moor, in North Yorkshire, for Class 5 training to enable her to fly four-engine heavy bombers. The conversion was done on the Handley Page Halifax, an aeroplane whose relationship to the Avro Lancaster was like that of the Hurricane to the Spitfire. A very capable aircraft, it was to serve in many other roles throughout the war but could never match the glamour of the Lancaster. Winnie flew three hours and forty minutes in the Halifax with her instructor, which would have involved general handling (steep turns, slow flying, stalls and so on) followed by circuits to get used to landing and taking off in various configurations.

Most importantly when learning to fly any multi-engine aircraft, she would have been taught how to handle asymmetric flight and landings following a simulated engine failure on one or two of the four engines.

Then she spent three hours and five minutes practising on her own. Not strictly 'on her own': ATA rules stipulated that when flying four-engine types (and, curiously, the twin-engine Douglas Dakota) pilots must be accompanied by a flight engineer. At the end of her course the Chief Flying Instructor reported she was a 'keen pilot of good average ability who flew the Halifax with confidence'. Lettice Curtis had been the first woman to fly an RAF four-engine bomber when she completed the conversion on a Halifax at the end of February 1943. In fact, only eleven female ATA pilots ever held the coveted Class 5 four-engine rating.

After being signed off Winnie returned to Aston Down. By the end of October she had logged seven hours and fifty-five minutes on the Avro Lancaster, which was powered by four 1,280 hp Rolls-Royce Merlins. At the opposite end of the scale she had also flown the little single-engine British

Taylorcraft Auster, a light liaison and observation aircraft with a 130 hp engine, as well as the twin-engine Bristol Beaufort torpedo-bomber developed from the Blenheim, and what the ATA described as 'Walrus types'. This category consisted of two aircraft. One was the ungainly-looking Supermarine Walrus amphibian which as the name suggests could be landed on sea or land, although the women of the ATA were not allowed to land on water. It was a biplane with a single engine mounted high above the fuselage in 'pusher' configuration, meaning the propeller pointed towards the tail. On land it waddled, but it was a very effective spotter aeroplane and air-sea rescue aircraft. The other aeroplane in the category was the Supermarine Sea Otter, intended as a replacement for the Walrus. It was very similar in design, except that the engine was more powerful and pointed forwards in conventional 'tractor' manner.

In November 1943 the Officer Commanding Number 9 Ferry Pool wrote on Winnie's general record,

> There has never been any question about her ability as a pilot or her record as a worker. Her sense of responsibility has improved, but I sometimes wonder whether her sense of duty does not occasionally waver.

The comments about her sense of duty may have arisen from a Disciplinary Offence Report, which states that on 4 October she had been suspended for a day with total loss of pay 'for contravening Standing Order C47' – whatever Standing Order C47 was.

Treasury rules meant that until 1943 women pilots in the ATA had been paid less than male pilots (£6 a week compared to £8 a week), but now that men and women were ferrying the same types Pauline Gower was able, in her quiet, determined way, to persuade the government to give the women equal pay. It was an important breakthrough, because it was the first time any government had ever agreed to pay men and women the same rate for the same job.

In 1942 the *Sketch* printed a double-page spread of excellent caricatures of many of the female pilots of the ATA. They were drawn by 'Sammy' Clayton (Edna Violet Clayton) who was herself an ATA pilot. Clayton captured Winnie in her dress uniform, characteristically seated on a bar stool, legs crossed, cigarette in her left hand and a glass of beer in her right. In contrast, a straightforward pastel portrait of a serious-looking Flight Captain Mrs. Winifred Crossley, sketched by Olive Snell, appeared in the

Tatler on 6 October 1943. The caption to it concluded with the news that 'She is engaged to Capt. Peter Fair of British Airways.'

* * *

After Peter Fair had recovered from ditching his Lockheed Super Electra in the Mediterranean in December 1939 he went back to work. Imperial Airways and British Airways merged to become British Overseas Airways Corporation (BOAC), which officially came into being in April 1940 and operated during the war as a nationalised airline flying international routes. Captain Fair flew for BOAC to the Far East and Africa. In September 1941 the Corporation inaugurated the North Atlantic Return Ferry service, using American Consolidated Liberators. Captain Peter Fair was one of the BOAC pilots who operated the service, which flew at least one aircraft per day each way. Depending on the weather, a flight could take up to 12 hours to complete. The B-24 Liberator was a four-engine heavy bomber with a massive H-tail, high cruising speed and long range. BOAC's Liberators had all the armament removed, provision for passenger seating and a revised cabin oxygen and heating system. Nobody had ever flown the North Atlantic in winter before, but BOAC managed to maintain a year-round two-way service between Prestwick and Montreal for the rest of the war.

At some point – in late 1941, perhaps – Winnie and Frank divorced, and in June 1942 Frank, now a major in the Royal Artillery, married again. In September 1943 Winnie and Peter Fair announced their engagement, when they were spending a golfing holiday in Ayrshire together. 'Captain Fair', reported the *Daily Record*, 'says that his bride-to-be is a better pilot than himself', the paper adding that she probably had more flying hours than any other woman in the world. That may well have been true. The marriage took place in London in December 1943. Now Mrs. Winifred Fair, she returned to her ferry duties and her husband to crossing and recrossing the Atlantic.

* * *

Throughout early 1944 the ATA was increasingly involved in the build up to the D-Day invasion. Winnie found herself doing less taxi work and flying more operational types. New to her were the Fairey Albacore, a biplane torpedo bomber, and the Fairey Barracuda monoplane torpedo bomber, the latter one of the most ungainly aeroplanes ever produced. Both were single-engine types. She also flew the twin-engine Douglas Dakota transport, used by the Allies throughout the war and one of the most successful designs in history.

A week before the D-Day landings Winnie was posted to Number 6 Ferry Pool at Ratcliffe, near Leicester. On leaving Aston Down the Commanding Officer of wrote that 'I have noticed a distinct improvement in her sense of duty. All the time she has been in No 9 FP she has worked very hard and well, and has done all that has been asked of her.'

No doubt gratified by these remarks, she started at Ratcliffe on 1 June 1944, and by September had flown the Grumman Hellcat, a tubby carrier-borne fighter, and the Stinson Reliant, a light communications aircraft, both single-engine American designs. Memorably she also flew four hours and twenty minutes in Short Stirlings, which had been the RAF's first four-engine bomber. A huge aeroplane with a stalky undercarriage, probably the best-known photograph of one shows it towering above Joan Hughes, one of the ATA's First Eight, who was standing beside a mainwheel. She is the same height as the tyre. Stirlings suffered operationally because they had too short a wingspan and could not fly high enough, the Air Ministry insisting that the wingspan should be no more than 100 feet in order to fit in a standard RAF hangar. By 1944 Stirlings were being used as glider tugs and transports.

Between September 1944 and January 1945 Winnie continued ferrying a wide variety of aircraft, but the only type new to her was the twin-engine North American B-25 Mitchell medium bomber which featured a tricycle undercarriage. In January 1945 permission was given to the women to ferry operational aircraft to France, Holland and Belgium. Winnie told a journalist in 1946 that 'after the second front was well established she went over to the continent', but it's not possible to tell which of the aircraft she flew between January 1945 and war's end in May 1945 were the ones she flew across the Channel. Perhaps not many of them, because in February 1945 she was posted to Number 4 Ferry Pool at Prestwick in Ayrshire. It would be nice to think that this was because her husband Peter Fair flew into and out of there with the BOAC Liberators of the North Atlantic Return Ferry service. Peter would have been able to brief Winnie about the flying characteristics of the Liberators she ferried while she was stationed at Prestwick. She also added the very large Grumman Avenger carrier-based torpedo bomber – the heaviest single-engine aircraft of the Second World War – to her list of types flown.

All flying training in the ATA had ceased before VE Day ('Victory in Europe') on 8 May 1945, and now the organisation was being run down and the Ferry Pools closed. Nevertheless Winnie Fair managed to fly a total of

82 hours and 10 minutes in the next five months. The Royal Navy's Fairey Firefly reconnaissance fighter was new to her, but the fifteen minutes she logged in the Grumman Wildcat naval fighter looks like an excuse to fly a new type while the opportunity was there.

It was the last new type she would fly with the ATA. The CO of Number 4 Ferry Pool wrote that she was 'A very good pilot and willing worker. Very popular with all pilots of her flight and shows great keenness in all the work of the Pool.'

That work was now over. On Saturday 29 September 1945 the ATA staged its final farewell at White Waltham airfield, the only time it put on a public performance. Some 12,000 people paid to see the show, the money raised going to the ATA Benevolent Fund to help to look after the families of the pilots who had lost their lives. The public were able to look over some of the many different aircraft the ATA had ferried during the war, and were treated to a flying display. Since ATA pilots did not hold a display rating the aircraft were flown by service pilots. Many of the women pilots had already left the ATA, but Lettice Curtis brought in a Liberator and it's not beyond the realms of possibility that Winnie was also there in some capacity. The final entry in her ATA record is typed in red ink and reads 'CONTRACT TERMINATED 30.11.45.' And that was that. After a dozen years of almost constant flying she was redundant.

* * *

During the near six-year existence of the Women's Section of the Air Transport Auxiliary, from 1 January 1940 until 30 November 1945, only three pilots served from the first day to the last. They were Joan Hughes, Rosemary Rees and Winnie. Both Rees and Hughes received MBEs for their wartime work.

According to her ferry records, Winnie flew 1,757 hours and 45 minutes with the ATA encompassing 44 different types. In reality it was many more types than that. The heading 'Moth variants' for example not only includes the Tiger Moth but also the Fox, Gipsy, Puss, Leopard and Hornet Moths, all of which were used by the ATA. Winnie herself said in an interview in early 1946 that she had flown '60 different types of military aircraft'.

In round figures Winnie flew 176 hours in those various Moths. She also amassed 897 hours, half of the hours she logged with the ATA, flying taxi aeroplanes (Oxford, Anson, Dominie/Rapide, Argus). Among the many other aircraft she flew she spent 58 hours ferrying Hurricanes; 45 hours flying Spitfires and Seafires; 52 hours on Wellingtons; 30 hours on Beaufighters; 84 hours flying Mosquitoes; 42 hours on the Halifax; 30 hours on Typhoons and 81 hours flying Lancasters.

It is important to understand that most ferry flights were of less than an hour's duration. For example, Hatfield to Cowley in a taxi Rapide would take 15 minutes, with the passengers getting out while the engines were running and the Rapide taking off again shortly afterwards. Even with a Lancaster, the ferry flight from the factory airfield in Manchester to a bomber airfield in Lincolnshire would perhaps take 40 minutes. Winnie's 81 hours on the Lancaster were probably made up of over 100 separate flights, each one in a different Lancaster. On the other hand, taking a Tiger Moth to Scotland would take hours and in winter would almost certainly entail an overnight stop on the way. All pilots know that no two take-offs, no two flights and particularly no two landings are ever the same. Flying is a tiring business because each flight is a separate challenge and demands full concentration.

Winnie was the first woman to fly a frontline RAF fighter (Hurricane), and one of only 11 women cleared to fly four-engine aircraft. Including her pre-war flying in Moths and Avro 504s and the like she left the ATA at the end of November with 3,617 hours and 45 minutes in her numerous logbooks. In the 1946 interview she claimed to have flown more than 4,000 hours, and in her entire flying career 'never had an accident or damaged an aircraft'. It was a slight and pardonable exaggeration. She was asked about flying in the future:

> Mrs. Fair said she 'was sure she couldn't stay from it long.' At the moment she is quite exhausted after six years of flying in the ATA. It was a life which meant uncomfortable billets on lonely stations, flying in cold and miserable winter weather and meals, such as they were, snatched at odd intervals.

The story appeared in several Canadian newspapers and included the news that Winifred Fair had 'arrived in Montreal by Clipper from England to be with her Canadian husband now residing in Montreal'. BOAC's Boeing 314 Clippers were long-range four-engine flying boats and flying in one was a new experience for her. In the ATA's classification flying boats were Class 6 aeroplanes, which women were not allowed to fly.

When she arrived in Canada she had just celebrated her fortieth birthday and for the time being had put post-war austerity Britain behind her. Few

ATA women pilots continued in aviation after the war, and there is no evidence that Winnie ever flew as a pilot again. There is no reason to doubt her claim that she was exhausted after six years of non-stop flying, but there was another factor that may have had a bearing on her decision. Because of the mighty effort put into military aviation during the war there had been no civil aviation to speak of in Britain, and now there were no modern aircraft and no infrastructure, few passengers and not much freight to be carried. When it did restart, post-war civilian flying had to use ex-military aircraft like the Avro Lancastrian, a converted Lancaster, and the Douglas Dakota. There were not many jobs, and those there were had a surplus of demobbed, highly-trained and experienced former RAF pilots chasing them.

Besides, Winnie had nothing more to prove.

Chapter Seven

Afterwards

Peter Fair continued flying the North Atlantic, no longer in BOAC's wartime Liberators but in the company's graceful four-engine Lockheed Constellation passenger aircraft, flying from New York or Montreal to London. By 1947 he had logged 8,500 hours, flown more than a million miles (becoming one of BOAC's 'Mileage Millionaires'), and had crossed the Atlantic 150 times. Winnie seems to have paid several visits by air to England, and in 1946 her son John, a 17-year-old student, crossed the Atlantic to visit his mother.

A terrible tragedy struck Winnie in 1950. To anyone who has not suffered a similar awful loss it is an unimaginable event. In the absence of imagination we must simply let the facts speak for themselves. The *Western Times* reported on 24 November 1950:

> The death of Mr. John Crossley has cast a gloom over local cricketing circles. Deceased was only about 22, and had been a playing member of the Bovey Tracey Cricket Club for some years. He lived at Harbertonford. His death came with tragic suddenness. He was at Bovey Tracey on Thursday night last, and not feeling very well, went to bed. Returning to his home, he became worse, and on Saturday was removed to Bovey hospital, where he died soon after admission. Only a fortnight ago he received the president's bat for being the best all-rounder for last season. Mr. Crossley was a nephew of Dr. John Harrison [sic] the president of Bovey Tracey Cricket Club.

* * *

In 1948 Winnie's younger sister Muriel had married at the age of 36. Her husband was a Pole named Edward Bartniczak, but he had died soon after. In 1950 Muriel then married Peter Fair's younger brother Alfred, who called himself Cleugh-Fair. The Cleugh part of Alfred's name was his mother's maiden name; the hyphen was Alfred's own invention.

Alfred Davidson Colin Cleugh-Fair was seven years younger that Peter. He followed in Peter's footsteps and joined the RAF as a pilot in 1934, moving on to flying boats as a junior pilot officer. In the RAF pilots were expected to be modest and self-effacing, and anyone who told exaggerated tales or boasted about themselves was known as a line-shooter. Alfred Cleugh-Fair was a line-shooter, a characteristic that perhaps explains his use of the hyphenated surname. Like his wife Muriel he had also been married before, in his case in 1940 to an Irish woman called Jessica Synge, daughter of Sir Francis and Lady Synge. They divorced in 1949. But the Cleugh-Fairs are not strictly part of Winnie's story, except to note the coincidence of two brothers marrying two sisters, and the fact that both brothers were involved in ditching an aeroplane into the sea, Alfred in 1937, and Peter in 1939.

In 1952 Winnie and Peter were living in Chawton, near Alton in Hampshire when they appeared in the *Tatler*, photographed at a ball held in Chawton House. Peter, 'a senior BOAC captain' is seen smiling and chatting to a young lady, while Winnie, in evening dress, a drink in her hand and with her characteristic broad smile, appears as one of a group of guests sitting on the stairs.

Peter Fair was still flying the North Atlantic routes. In 1949 the beautiful Lockheed Constellations had been replaced by ungainly Boeing 377 Stratocruisers, which were derived from wartime B-29 bombers. With a fuselage cross-section shaped like a figure eight the Stratocruiser was the ultimate in luxury travel and completely uneconomical to operate.

By January 1955 Peter had logged over 13,000 flying hours, flown two-and-a-half million miles and crossed the Atlantic nearly 400 times. As one of BOAC's most experienced captains he was chosen by the national flag-carrier to fly 24-year-old Princess Margaret on her first official 'solo' visit abroad, a tour of the Caribbean that aroused worldwide interest and not a little criticism. The newsreels recorded the departure of BOAC Stratocruiser Canopus from London Airport on 31 January 1955, seen off by the Queen, the Duke of Edinburgh, the Queen Mother and members of the Cabinet. The aircraft refuelled at freezing Montreal, then landed to refuel again at Montego Bay in Jamaica, before making the final 900-mile flight to Trinidad, where the newsreel cameras recorded Peter Fair's landing and the Princess shaking hands with the crew after exiting the aircraft. They collected her from Bermuda a month later and flew her back to a cold and foggy London Airport to be met by members of the Royal family, more handshakes and more newsreel cameras.

Peter and Winnie both turned 50 in 1956. That may have been one of the reasons why Peter accepted the position of General Manager of Bahamas Airways Limited, a wholly-owned and wholly loss-making subsidiary of BOAC which employed 55 staff. Another may have been the chance to live and work in a tropical paradise. Situated in the Atlantic, north of Cuba and east of the Florida Keys, the Bahamas comprised more than 700 islands which were then a British colony. Bahamas Airways was based in the capital Nassau, on the island of New Providence. It flew inter-island services as well as serving Florida, using three amphibians (two Grumman Goose aircraft and a war-surplus Consolidated Catalina) and three de Havilland DH 114 Heron airliners.

One of the pilots employed by Bahamas Airways was Ed Ballard, an American who had joined the ATA in June 1941. Ballard had married Ruth Lambton, a British pilot who joined the ATA in the summer of 1940. Like Winnie, the Ballards had reached Class 5 and were able to ferry four-engine bombers. They were both dismissed from the ATA in January 1945 for 'unauthorised drinking', with Ruth additionally found guilty of insubordination. They were friendly with Lettice Curtis and invited her to stay with them in Nassau over Christmas 1957. Lettice was one of the few ATA women who remained in aviation after the war. When she arrived at Windsor Field, Nassau, two days before Christmas in pouring rain and gales, she was met by Winnie and Ruth Ballard. She wrote in her autobiography that Peter Fair had arranged for her to fly as second pilot in any Bahamas Airways aeroplane during her visit, but to make things legal she had to be issued with a ticket for each flight showing a 100 per cent rebate.

She flew with Ed Ballard in a Grumman Goose amphibian, made two flights with him in the Heron and had two trips in the Catalina, but her most memorable flight was in a Grumman Goose to Harbour Island with pilot Bill Quick. Winnie went along as a passenger: her friends Lois and Alan Butler had a house on the island and Winnie went over from time to time to check on it. Lettice Curtis relates that the Grumman Goose developed engine problems but made it safely to land on the water at Harbour Island. A dinghy was sent out to take Winnie and her maid off:

> Once the aircraft was safely ashore Bill and I disembarked to join Winnie. By now she had walked up to the house and we found her walking round the garden with the gardener, who had just been asked to cut down a large bunch of bananas for her to take back to Nassau. In the evening we walked downtown

to a small restaurant where a pianist, who during the summer worked in Majorca, played to us while we ate.

When we got back to the house after dinner, Bill and I walked in the dark round the island, famous for its pink sands. Somehow we all found somewhere to sleep in the empty house. When I woke in the morning I decided that a cup of tea would go down well; but there was no tea, and all I could find were tins of beer, so I took them round instead!

The next day they were rescued by a Grumman Widgeon and flown back to Nassau. Curtis prints a photograph taken on 28 December 1957 at the Pilot House Club in Nassau. Four middle-aged ladies are seated around a table on a patio, facing the camera and awaiting their lunch. On the left is Ann Wood-Kelly, an American who flew with the ATA. Next to her is Lettice Curtis, with what looks suspiciously like a half-smile on her lips. Then comes Ruth Ballard, and lastly, to the right, is Winnie with a dachshund on her lap and a glass in her hand. Winnie is smiling happily. The lifestyle and the climate obviously suited her very well.

During his first three years as General Manager Peter Fair expanded and reorganised the airline, adding new services and upgrading the fleet. Then late in 1958 BOAC sold 80 per cent of its shareholding to another airline operating in the Bahamas. Peter stayed on. But private enterprise could no more make a profit than BOAC and in December 1960 Peter Fair called a press conference in his office to announce that the company 'had been floundering, had been losing money and many matters were not as they should be', and that BOAC was retaking control of Bahamas Airways.

Winnie and Peter had visited England in the summer of 1960, staying with the Butlers at Studham Hall Farm, their home near Dunstable from where Winnie had towed gliders in an Avro 504 twenty-two years earlier, in a long-vanished pre-war world. They returned to Nassau on the S.S. *Reina del Mar* cruise ship operating out of Southampton to the western coast of South America. Peter's occupation was given on the passenger manifest as 'Airline Executive' and Winnie's as 'housewife'.

At some point, possibly in early 1961, Peter was diagnosed with lung cancer. He died in the Chester County Hospital, West Chester, Pennsylvania on 24 November 1961. He was just 55.

* * *

Winnie returned to England. She took a house called Fox Meadow in Potten End, near Berkhamsted in Hertfordshire, probably because it was close to the Butlers at Studham. She kept dogs, including a Labrador, played golf and by 1966 was living with a man called Alan Borton, who was fifteen years her junior. He had been born in India in 1921, the son of an officer in the Royal Engineers. He attended Bedford School, before serving from 1940 to 1946 with the Gurkha Rifles in India, Italy and the Middle East. After the war he read Modern Languages at King's College, Cambridge, later qualifying as a solicitor before becoming a financial consultant. Winnie's niece Diana Scott remembers him being very shy. She also recalls that Winnie characteristically gave names to her cars. In the sixties she had a two-tone black and white Vauxhall called Whisky, after the Black and White whisky brand, and later a Ford Capri called Gracie, after Gracie Fields who lived on the island of Capri. At the end of the 1970s she and Alan Borton moved to a house not far away called The Swallows in Dagnall, near Berkhamsted.

Winnie died on 27 March 1984 at the age of 78. After her death Alan Borton told her brother George that he wished he had married her. Four years later he did get married, to a woman called Edith Koessler. He died in September 1995.

* * *

Winifred Mary Harrisson, the daughter of a famous doctor, who became Mrs. Winifred Crossley and then Mrs. Winifred Fair, deserves to be remembered for her considerable achievements as a pioneer airwoman. She learned to fly at a time when few women did, and by practising hard became an accomplished aerobatic pilot. She became the first professional aerobatic pilot in the country (and possibly in the world) when she joined C. W. A. Scott's Flying Display and toured the British Isles. After that adventure she earned a living as a commercial pilot, mostly towing banners and gliders.

With 1,860 hours in her logbook when war broke out she was a hugely experienced pilot, and when the Women's Section of the Air Transport Auxiliary was set up she was one of the first eight women invited to join. During her six years' service she spent a further 1,758 hours flying the ATA's taxi aeroplanes or ferrying the RAF's and the Royal Navy's aircraft. She was the first woman ever to fly a frontline RAF fighter, and one of a handful of women who were qualified to fly four-engine heavy bombers. She served in the ATA's Women's Section from its first day until the last. When the curtain came down on the ATA at the end of November 1945 she had flown many hundreds of aeroplanes and roughly sixty different types.

She achieved more than most and deserves to be remembered and celebrated. Unfortunately, she didn't write her memoirs and her logbooks have disappeared. She died just before the resurgence of interest in the 168 women who flew with the ATA, a fascination that grows as time passes. As a result, other women pilots who achieved far less, but who lived longer or wrote books about their experiences, or had books written about them or were interviewed for television programmes, have received the adulation of an admiring press and public.

In September 2008 the British government finally acknowledged the role of the ATA during the war when surviving pilots were awarded a special Veterans' Badge at a ceremony held in 10 Downing Street. By then Winnie had been dead for almost a quarter of a century.

The Royal Mail issued a set of stamps in 2022 to commemorate the work of women during the Second World War. Four of the stamps were collectively called *Spitfire Women – Ferry Pilots of the Air Transport Auxiliary*. Of the photographs chosen to represent the Women's Section, two show the glamour girls of the ATA: socialite Diana Barnato Walker, whose millionaire father owned the Bentley Motor Company, and the much-photographed Maureen Dunlop. Another stamp has a well-known photograph of a group of women pilots emerging from an Avro Anson, led by Pauline Gower and including Joan Hughes, Margaret Cunnison and Margaret Fairweather of the First Eight. The fourth photograph is of Faith Bennett in the cockpit of a Lockheed Hudson. Winnie does not feature on the stamps. Today she is almost forgotten.

But not quite. In 2019 the Hertfordshire bus company Uno named eight of their buses after the First Eight women to join the ATA in tribute to what it rightly called 'a very special sisterhood'. Fittingly, *Winifred Crossley* and the other named buses run on the company's route 653 between St. Albans, Hatfield and Welwyn Garden City.

And in October 2021 Barnet Council ran an online poll to name 'the square outside Barnet Council's Colindale office'. Voters were asked to choose between four of the First Eight ATA women pilots. The choice lay between Crossley Square, Fairweather Square, Friedlander Square and Patterson Square. There were 344 votes cast. Mona Friedlander received 6 per cent, Winifred Crossley Fair 18 per cent, Margaret Fairweather 36 per cent and Gabrielle Patterson 41 per cent. Although it is now officially called Patterson Square, the council's website is careful to say it 'also celebrates the contribution made by all female pilots'.

Winnie would have been highly amused at having her name on the front of a bright pink and blue 'Tiger Moth' bus, and at nearly having a square named after her. As a pilot she was highly-skilled and treated flying as a deadly serious business, but away from the cockpit she lived life to the full with a smile on her face, a glass in her hand and a cigarette in her fingers. She was vivacious, outgoing, amusing, warm, generous, charming and, I suspect, too busy having fun to have cared very much what posterity thought of her.

Acknowledgements

It's no exaggeration to say that without the help, encouragement and enthusiasm of Winnie Crossley's niece Diana Scott this book would not have been written. Not only was she happy to give me her personal recollections of her aunt, she also allowed me to borrow and scan her numerous Harrisson family photographs and Winnie's Royal Aero Club Aviator's Certificate. Diana's kindness further extended to reading this book in draft form and giving me her thoughts on it, as did the late Barbara Dickerson, Andrew Neville and Jenni Brown, to whom my thanks are also due.

Penny Cheshire, who is also Winnie's niece, generously allowed me to see and to scan her photographs and a marvellous portrait of Winnie on silk. I am likewise in her debt.

Terry Mace has created a website about the golden age of interwar flying which is both outstanding and comprehensive. He also maintains another wonderful website which commemorates the men and women pilots of the Air Transport Auxiliary. He has been extraordinarily generous in sharing his material. To give but one example, Winnie's Air Transport Auxiliary records were unavailable to view during the Covid pandemic but Terry sent me the photographs he had taken of them before lockdown. And if that was not enough, he also read the draft manuscript and gave me his observations on it. I'm very grateful to him for all his help.

My thanks are due to Simon Bates of The Mallowry at Riseley for sharing the history of the house he put together from the title deeds relating to the property. Peter Wright, David Allen and the members of Gamlingay and District History Society have once again given me unfailing assistance and support.

It would be remiss of me not to thank Amy Jordan, my ever-helpful and ever-patient editor at Pen and Sword Books, for guiding me through the process of getting this book into print.

And equally remiss of me not mention Rex Whitfield, who is always ready to share his extensive knowledge of family and local history and to give sound advice, from which I have benefited over more years than either of us care to remember.

The Uno bus company very kindly supplied a photograph of the bus they have dedicated to Winnie Crossley, for which I am most grateful.

I am of course deeply indebted to my wife Debbie for her boundless support and her firm belief that Winnie's story should be better known than it is. Without her, the research, writing and publication of this book would not have happened.

Finally, I must point out that any errors in it are entirely my own fault.

List of Illustrations

Publicity postcard printed for Captain Percival Phillips: *Courtesy Gamlingay and District History Society*
Winnie with an Air Publicity Avro 504N: *Courtesy Diana Scott*
Winnie in flying helmet and goggles: *Courtesy Diana Scott*
Six of the first eight women to join the ATA at Hatfield, 10 January 1940: *© Illustrated London News Ltd./Mary Evans*
Pauline Gower at the piano in March 1940: *© Illustrated London News Ltd./Mary Evans*
Portrait of Winnie by Olive Snell: *© Illustrated London News Ltd./Mary Evans*
Winnie and her mother in 1942: *Courtesy Diana Scott*
Wedding group 1945: *Courtesy Diana Scott*
Hawker Hurricane, Supermarine Spitfire and Dragon Rapide: *Author*
Consolidated Liberator: *icholokov/iStock*
Winnie and Lois Butler: *© Illustrated London News Ltd./Mary Evans*
Winnie in the Bahamas: *Courtesy Diana Scott*
Air Publicity's G-ADEV, restored as an Avro 504K and still flying: *Author*
On a beach in the Bahamas: *Courtesy Diana Scott*
With her dogs: *Courtesy Diana Scott*
The Harrisson siblings: *Courtesy Diana Scott*

C. W. A. Scott's Flying Display 1936 Itinerary

This itinerary has been compiled using the partial listing in *Those Fabulous Flying Years: Joy-Riding and Flying Circuses Between the Wars* by Colin Cruddas (Air-Britain, Tonbridge, 2003), numerous newspaper reports, *Flight* magazine and other sources. It's likely that further displays took place during August, probably in the west country.

7 April	Ace of Spades/Hook airfield
9 April	Chesham, Ley Green Road
10 April	Dorking, Great Bookham, Bagden Hill
11 April	Redhill
12, 13 April	Barnet, Bailey's Farm, Mays Lane
16 April	Thetford
17 April	Bury St Edmunds
18 April	Slough
19 April	Witley
20 April	Burgess Hill
21 April	Billingshurst
22 April	Swindon
23 April	Dorchester
24 April	Taunton
25 April	Torrington
26 April	Exeter
27 April	Frome
28 April	Shepton Mallet
29 April	Bristol
30 April	Malvern
1 May	Towcester
2 May	Leicester, Braunceston

3 May	Nottingham
4 May	Lichfield
6 May	Derby
7 May	Stoke
8 May	Llangefni
10 May	Dublin, Phoenix Park
11 May	Dublin, Raheny
12 May	Maryborough
13 May	Longford, Clooncoose Racecourse
14 May	Athlone, Big Meadow
15 May	Thurles
16 May	Cobh
17 May	Cork, Farmers Cross
18 May	Dungarvan
19 May	Mallow
20 May	Fermoy, ex RAF aerodrome
21 May	Clonmel
22 May	Tralee, The Racecourse
23 May	Newcastle West
24 May	Limerick, Banemore, Ballycummin
25 May	Kilkenny, Dunmore
26 May	Temperlaney, Arklow
27 May	Wexford, Coolpeach, Drinagh
28 May	Waterford, Kilcohen Park Racecourse
29 May	Wicklow, Silver Strand, Kilpole
30 May	Dundalk, Marsh Farm, Dublin Road
31 May	Drogheda, Church Field, Mornington
1 June	Lurgan, Townland
2 June	Ballymena, Upper Broughshane
3 June	Belfast, Newtonards, Ards Aerodrome
4 June	Coleraine, Old Lodge Road
5 June	Londonderry, Coolkeeragh
6 June	Omagh, Strathroy, ex-RAF aerodrome
7 June	Sligo, Scardenmore, Stranhill Road
8 June	Ballymore, Boyle
9 June	Castlebar, ex-RAF aerodrome
10 June	Ballinrobe, Tuam Racecourse

11 June	Galway, Oranmore Aerodrome
12 June	Ennis, Castleclare
13 June	Ballinrobe, Tuam Racecourse
14 June	Nenagh, Knockalton Lane
15 June	Lewistown, Naas
16 June	Enniscorthy, Hollyfort House
17 June	Carlow, Old Racecourse
18 June	Dublin, Leopardstown Racecourse
19 June	Llanfairfechan
20, 21 June	Birmingham
24 June	Long Eaton, Wilsthorpe Flying Field
25 June	Bakewell *cancelled by the Air Ministry, field unsuitable*
26 June	Manchester, Timperley
27, 28 June	Liverpool, Huyton
29 June	Northwich, Wincham, Rose Farm
30 June	Birkenhead, Heswall, Irby Hall Farm
1, 2, 3, 4 July	Blackpool
5 July	Airdrie
6 July	Kirkintilloch, Easter Cadder Farm
7 July	Carnoustie
8 July	Aberdeen, Seaton
9 July	St Andrews
10 July	Anstruther
11 July	Perth
12 July	Kirkaldy
13 July	Auchterarder
14 July	North Berwick
15 July	Edinburgh, Corstophine, Tram terminus
16 July	Kilmarnock
18, 19 July	Wakefield, Bretton Park
20 July	Walsingham, Warham
22 July	Southwold
23 July	Great Yarmouth
25, 26 July	Norwood, Ewell, Nonsuch Park
27 July	Sandwich, Richborough Castle Farm
28 July	Folkestone, Capel–le–Ferne
31 July	Hastings, Church Farm, Fairlight *abandoned due to bad weather*

9 August	Newquay
10 August	Penzance/Rosevidney
13 August	Lynmoor, Lynton, Devon
14, 15 August	Weston Super Mare
23 August	Manchester, Reddish
23 August	Brighouse
	Sherburn-in-Elmet *unknown date in August*
27 August	Hull, Hedon
28 August	Sutton-on-Sea
1 September	Belfast, Old Aerodrome, Malone *cancelled due to fog delaying the Irish Sea crossing from Blackpool*
2 September	Belfast
3 September	Bangor
4 September	Ballymena
5 September	Strabane
7 September	Limavady
8 September	Portrush
9 September	Enniskillen
10 September	Lurgan
11 September	Antrim
12 September	Armagh, Farmacaffley
18 September	Sherborne, Warwick
19, 20 September	Solihull

A Receiver was appointed on 23 September.

Aircraft Types Flown

This is a list of aircraft that Winnie Crossley is known to have flown or probably flew during her twelve years as a pilot. There may well have been more. For instance, three Avro 640 Cadets were used by C.W.A. Scott's Flying Display as joy-riding aeroplanes, and it is more than likely that Winnie would have flown one of them at some time.

The aircraft marked with an asterisk are ones she probably flew. Her Air Transport Auxiliary records tend to group together similar types, such as 'Moth variant' and 'Wellington types'. As well as the Moths she is recorded as flying, the ATA is known to have used Puss, Leopard and Hornet Moths as taxi aeroplanes and the probability is that Winnie would have flown each of them at some point. There were only two types of Wellington produced (as opposed to sub-types), the Wellington itself and the Warwick which was developed from it. Again, she almost certainly flew both of them.

For military types the date given after 'Entered service' is when the aircraft entered service with the British. For civilian types the date given after 'Introduced' refers to when the first aeroplanes off the production line were sold. A specific mark or marks given in brackets after the engine details means those details refer to those marks only.

Airspeed Courier: Civilian five or six-seat light transport aircraft. Engine: one 305 hp Armstrong Siddeley Cheetah radial. Introduced 1933. Only 16 were built.

Airspeed Oxford: Trainer and communications aircraft. Engines: two 375 hp Armstrong Siddeley Cheetah radials (Oxford Mks. I and II). Entered service 1937.

Armstrong Whitworth Albemarle: Transport/glider tug. Engines: two 1,590 hp Bristol Hercules radials. Entered service 1943.

Armstrong Whitworth Whitley: Long-range bomber. Engines: two 1,145 hp Rolls-Royce Merlins. Entered service 1937.

Avro 504N: Trainer. Avro 504s were powered by several different engines, but Air Publicity's 504Ns had a 180 hp Armstrong Siddeley Lynx radial engine. Entered service 1914. Quickly obsolete as a frontline aircraft, Avro 504s were the standard RAF trainer until 1933.

Avro Anson: Trainer/communications aircraft. Engines: two 350 hp Armstrong Siddeley Cheetah radials (Anson Mk. I). Entered service 1936. Some 11,000 were built, the last in 1952.

Avro Lancaster: Long-range heavy bomber. Engines: four 1,640 hp Rolls-Royce Merlins (Lancaster Mk. I). Entered service 1942.

Bristol Beaufighter: Two-seat night-fighter, long-range fighter, anti-shipping strike fighter. Engines: two 1,670 hp Bristol Hercules radials (Beaufighter Mk. VI). Entered service 1940.

Bristol Beaufort: Torpedo bomber. Engines: two 1,130 hp Bristol Taurus radials. Entered service 1940.

Bristol Blenheim: Light bomber/trainer/night-fighter. Engines: two 905 hp Bristol Mercury radials. Entered service 1937.

British Taylorcraft Auster: Light liaison/observation aircraft. Engine: one 130 hp Lycoming (Auster Mk. V). Entered service 1942. British licence-built versions of the American Taylorcraft models.

Consolidated B-24 Liberator: American long-range bomber/transport/anti-submarine aircraft. Engines: four 1,200 hp Pratt & Whitney Twin Wasp radials. Entered service 1941.

De Havilland DH 60 Cirrus II Moth: Two-seat biplane light aircraft. Engine: one 85 hp ADC. Introduced 1927.

De Havilland DH 60G Gipsy Moth: Two-seat biplane light aircraft. Engine: one 100 hp de Havilland Gipsy. Introduced 1927.

De Havilland DH 80A Puss Moth:* Three-seat light aircraft. Engine: one 130 hp de Havilland Gipsy Major. Introduced 1930.

De Havilland DH 82A Tiger Moth: Two-seat biplane trainer. Engine: one 130 hp de Havilland Gipsy Major. Introduced 1934.

De Havilland DH 83 Fox Moth: Five-seat biplane light aircraft. Engine: one 130 hp de Havilland Gipsy Major. Introduced 1932.

De Havilland DH 85 Leopard Moth:* Three-seat light aircraft. Engine: one 130 hp de Havilland Gipsy Major. Introduced 1933.

De Havilland DH 87 Hornet Moth:* Three-seat light aircraft. Engine: one 130 hp de Havilland Gipsy Major. Introduced 1935.

De Havilland DH 89 Rapide/Dominie: six to eight-seat biplane airliner/ trainer. Engines: two 200 hp de Havilland Gipsy Queens. Introduced 1934.

De Havilland DH 90 Dragonfly: five-seat biplane luxury touring aircraft. Engines: two 142 hp de Havilland Gipsy Majors. Introduced 1936.

De Havilland DH 98 Mosquito: Multi-role two-seat bomber/fighter-bomber/night fighter/maritime strike/photo-reconnaissance aircraft. Engines: two 1,460 hp Rolls-Royce Merlins (Mosquito NF Mk. XVII). Entered service 1941.

Douglas Dakota: American troop carrier/freight/transport/glider tug. Engines: two 1,200 hp Pratt & Whitney Twin Wasp radials. Entered service 1941.

Douglas Boston:* American fighter/bomber/night-fighter/reconnaissance aircraft. Engines: two 1,200 hp Pratt & Whitney Twin Wasp radials (Boston Mks. I and II). Entered service 1940. Night-fighter versions were known as Havocs.

Fairchild Argus: American light transport/communication aircraft. Engine: one 165 hp Warner Scarab radial (Argus Mks. I and II) or one 200 hp Fairchild Ranger (Argus Mk. III). Entered service 1941.

Fairey Albacore: Carrier-borne biplane torpedo bomber. Engine: one 1,130 hp Bristol Taurus radial. Entered service 1940.

Fairey Barracuda: Carrier-borne torpedo and dive bomber. Engine: one 1,640 hp Rolls-Royce Merlin. Entered service 1943.

Fairey Battle: Light bomber/target tug. Engine: one 1,030 hp Rolls Royce Merlin. Entered service 1937.

Fairey Firefly: Carrier-borne reconnaissance fighter/fighter bomber. Engine: one 1,730 hp Rolls-Royce Griffon. Entered service 1943.

Grumman Avenger: American carrier-borne torpedo bomber. Engine: one 1,700 hp Wright Double Cyclone radial. Entered service 1943. The heaviest single-engine aeroplane of the Second World War.

Grumman Hellcat: American carrier-borne fighter. Engine: one 2,000 hp Pratt & Whitney Double Wasp radial. Entered service 1943.

Grumman Wildcat: American carrier-borne fighter/fighter-bomber. Engine: one 1,200 hp Pratt & Whitney Twin Wasp radial. Entered service 1940. Known as the Martlet by the British.

Handley Page Hampden: Medium bomber. Engines: two 1,000 hp Bristol Pegasus radials. Entered service 1938.

Handley Page Halifax: Long-range heavy bomber/transport/glider tug. Engines: four 1,615 hp Bristol Hercules radials (B.Mk. III). Entered service 1940.

Hawker Audax: * Two-seat Army co-operation biplane. Engine: one 530 hp Rolls-Royce Kestrel. Entered service 1932.

Hawker Demon: * Two-seat biplane fighter. Engine: one 485 hp Rolls-Royce Kestrel. Entered service 1931.

Hawker Hart: Two-seat biplane day bomber/trainer. Engine: one 525 hp Rolls-Royce Kestrel. Entered service 1930.

Hawker Hind:* Two-seat biplane light bomber/trainer. Engine: one 640 hp Rolls-Royce Kestrel. Entered service 1935.

Hawker Hurricane: Single-seat fighter/fighter-bomber. Engine: one 1,030 hp Rolls-Royce Merlin (Hurricane Mk.I). Entered service 1937.

Hawker Typhoon: Single-seat fighter-bomber. Engine: one 2,180 hp Napier Sabre. Entered service 1941.

Lockheed Hudson: American bomber/reconnaissance/utility aircraft. Engines: two 1,100 hp Wright Cyclone radials (Hudson Mks. I and II). Entered service 1939. Based on the Lockheed 14 Super Electra civil airliner.

Lockheed Ventura: American bomber/reconnaissance aircraft. Engines: two 2,000 hp Pratt & Whitney Double Wasp radials. Entered service 1942.

Miles Magister: The RAF's first monoplane two-seat trainer. Engine: one 130 hp de Havilland Gipsy Major. Entered service 1937.

Miles Master: Two-seat advanced trainer. Engine: one 870 hp Bristol Mercury radial (Master Mk. II). Entered service 1939.

North American B-25 Mitchell: American medium bomber. Engines: two 1,850 hp Wright Cyclone radials. Entered service 1943.

North American Harvard: American trainer. Engine: one 600 hp Pratt & Whitney Wasp radial. Entered service 1939.

North American Mustang: American long-range escort fighter and ground attack aircraft. Engine: one 1,520 hp Rolls-Royce Merlin (Mustang Mk. III). Entered service 1942.

Percival Proctor: Trainer/communications aircraft. Engine: one 210 hp de Havilland Gipsy Queen. Entered service 1940.

Short Stirling: Heavy bomber/transport/glider tug. Engines: four 1,650 hp Bristol Hercules radials (Stirling Mk. III). Entered service 1940.

Stinson Reliant: American light transport/communications aircraft. Engine: one 280 hp Lycoming. Entered service 1942.

Supermarine Sea Otter:* Biplane communications/air-sea rescue amphibian. Engine: one 855 hp Bristol Mercury radial. Entered service 1943.

Supermarine Spitfire/Seafire: Single-seat fighter/fighter-bomber/carrier-borne fighter. Engine: one 1,470 hp Rolls-Royce Merlin (Spitfire Mk. VB). Entered service 1938. Nearly 23,000 Spitfires of all marks were built.

Supermarine Walrus: Biplane reconnaissance/air-sea rescue amphibian. Engine: one 775 hp Bristol Pegasus radial (Walrus Mk. II). Entered service 1936.

Vickers Warwick:* Air-sea rescue reconnaissance/transport aircraft. Engines: two 2,500 hp Bristol Centaurus radials (Warwick GR.II). Entered service 1943.

Vickers Wellington: Long-range night-bomber. Engines: two 1,050 hp Bristol Pegasus radials (Wellington Mk. I). Entered service 1938.

Westland Lysander: Army co-operation/target tug/air-sea rescue/special operations aircraft. Engine: one 870 hp Bristol Mercury radial (Lysander Mk. III). Entered service 1938.

Westland Whirlwind: single-seat long-range fighter-bomber. Engines: two 885 hp Rolls-Royce Peregrines. Entered service 1940.

Bibliography

Chapman, W. E., *Cornwall Aviation Company* (Glasney Press, Falmouth, 1979).

Cheesman, E. C., *Brief Glory: The Story of the Air Transport Auxiliary* (1946, Maidenhead Heritage Trust reprint, 2008).

Cobham, Sir A. J., *A Time to Fly* (Shepheard-Walwyn, London, 1978).

Cruddas, C., *Those Fabulous Flying Years: Joy-Riding and Flying Circuses Between the Wars* (Air-Britain, Tonbridge, 2003).

Cruddas, C., *Sir Alan Cobham*: *Flying Legend Who Brought Aviation to the Masses* (Frontline Books, Yorkshire, 2018).

Curtis, L., *Lettice Curtis: Her Autobiography* (Red Kite, Walton on Thames, 2004).

Ellis, M., and Foreman, M., *A Spitfire Girl: One of the World's Greatest Female ATA Ferry Pilots Tells Her Story – Mary Ellis* (Frontline Books, Yorkshire, 2016).

Gower, P., *Women With Wings* (John Long, London, 1938).

Gunston, W., *The Illustrated Directory of Fighting Aircraft of World War II* (Salamander Books, London, 2001).

Jackson, A. J., *De Havilland Aircraft since 1909* (Third Edition, Putnam, London, 1987).

King, A., *Golden Wings: The Story of Some of the Women Ferry Pilots of the Air Transport Auxiliary* (C. Arthur Pearson, London, 1956).

Mason, T., *British Flight Testing: Martlesham Heath, 1920-1939*, (Putnam, London, 1993).

Mason, T., *The Secret Years: Flight Testing at Boscombe Down, 1939-1945* (Hikoki Publications, Aldershot, 1998).

Monday, D., *The Hamlyn Concise Guide to British Aircraft of World War II* (Hamlyn, London, 1982).

Ogilvy, D., *Shuttleworth: The Historic Aeroplanes* (Airlife, Shrewsbury, 1989).

Volkersz, V., *The Sky and I* (W. H. Allen, London, 1956).

Welch, A., *Happy to Fly: An Autobiography* (John Murray, London, 1983).

Wheeler, J., *The Hurricane Girls: The inspirational true story of the women who dared to fly* (Penguin, London, 2018).

Whittell, G., *Spitfire Women of World War II* (Harper Perennial, London, 2007).

Winchester, C., ed., *Wonders of World Aviation, Volumes I and II* (The Fleetwood House, London, 1938). Originally published by the Amalgamated Press as 40 part works.

Magazines

The Illustrated Encyclopedia of Aircraft, a partwork in 18 volumes (London, 1981–1985).

Flight [*Flight International* since 1962] (London, 1909–).

Aeroplane Monthly (London 1973–). An article by Lettice Curtis, *Anything To Anywhere*, about the ATA, was serialised in the *Aeroplane Monthly* issues for January, February, March and April 1979.

Websites

www.afleetingpeace.org
Terry Mace's site devoted to the pilots of the golden age of interwar flying.

www.ata-ferry-pilots.org
Terry Mace's site commemorating all the male and female pilots of the Air Transport Auxiliary.

https://atamuseum.org
The Air Transport Auxiliary Museum and Archive has an excellent collection of photographs, logbooks and other items related to the organisation.

Sources

P ublished works listed in the bibliography are given here under the surname of the author and the shortened title

Part One: County Set

Page 1: **The poet Robert Frost**: Robert Frost's poem *The Road Not Taken* was published in 1916.

Page 1: **It may have happened at Huntingdon**: The itineraries of the Number One and Number Two tours of Cobham's National Aviation Day displays in 1933 are in Cruddas, *Those Fabulous Flying Years*, pages 117–8.

Page 1: **Wyboston had been well-publicised in advance**: For example, publicity in the form of an advertisement and Cobham's press release appeared in the *Bedfordshire Times and Independent*, 9 June 1933.

Page 2: **the *Bedfordshire Times and Independent***: A brief report of the display appeared in the *Bedfordshire Times and Independent*, 16 June 1933.

Page 2: **she later told a journalist that it was going up for *flights* with Cobham**: *Luton News*, 25 May 1939.

Page 2: **She told another reporter in 1936 that 'I visited an air display'**: *Waterford Standard*, 30 May 1936.

Page 2: **Winnie was born Winifred Mary Harrisson on 9 January 1906 in St Neots**: The St Neots baptism register gives her actual date of birth, as does her Royal Aero Club Aviator's Certificate.

Page 2: Ernest studied medicine, graduating from Clare College: Obituary of Dr E. H. Harrisson in the *British Medical Journal*, 10 January 1942. For the four Harrisson brothers at Cambridge see *Alumni Cantabrigienses*, Volume 2 Part 3. Edited by J. Venn and J. A. Venn (Cambridge, 1947). Other details of the Harrisson family in St Neots are taken from *Kelly's Directory of Huntingdonshire* 1910 and 1914; the 1911 and the 1921 Census; and the 1939 Register (*findmypast.co.uk* accessed 24 November 2019).

Page 3: stated that she had been educated at Burchett House School: ATA Application Form, 1st December 1939: RAF Museum ATA/1906-01-09/CrossleyW.

Page 3: In 1921 Winnie and her twin sister Daphne were at another boarding school for girls: 1921 Census.

Page 4: The *Biggleswade Chronicle* noted that the tennis tournament: *Biggleswade Chronicle*, 10 July 1925.

Page 4: Frank's great-grandfather James Crossley: A study of the Crossley family in Ripley is on the Ripley and District Heritage Trust website at *www.rdht.org.uk* (accessed 5 November 2021).

Page 4: Bertram Crossley was an enthusiastic member of the local Territorial Army: e.g., *Ripley and Heanor News*, 10 November 1906; *Sheffield Daily Telegraph*, 24 February 1908; *Derbyshire Advertiser*, 5 September 1914.

Page 4: His death certificate gave the cause of death as epilepsy: *www. rdht.org.uk* (accessed 5 November 2021).

Page 4: the school magazine, *The Malvernian*, record that he represented the school: e.g., *The Malvernian*, June 1922, November 1922, March 1923.

Page 4: A photograph of the Malvern football team: *Illustrated Sporting and Dramatic News*, 18 February 1922.

Page 5: obtained a Bachelor of Arts degree: He is described as 'James Francis Crossley Esq., B.A.' in a 1927 lease (information supplied by Simon Bates).

Page 5: He played football for the University: *The Sportsman*, 9 November 1923.

Page 5: she and Frank were married: In its report of the wedding, the *Peterborough Standard* of 10 September 1926 included the news that 'Mr. and Mrs. Crossley left at 4 o'clock for London, and are flying to Italy for the honeymoon'.

Page 5: It was called The Mallowry: The present owner of the house, Simon Bates, very kindly supplied a history of it taken from the legal documents; *Electoral Register*, Riseley, 1930; property details and photographs advertised on 25 June 2020 at *www.facebook.com/MGliving/posts/the-mallowry-in-riseley-bedfordshire-is-an-edwardian-five-bedroom-detached-cape-/2618371781747735/* (accessed 20 April 2022).

Page 5: there was a tennis court: When the contents of the house were auctioned by W. & H. Peacock in February 1927, lots included lawn mowers and 'Tennis Posts and Net', *Bedfordshire Times and Independent* 4 February 1927.

Page 5: Two of Winnie's uncles played Minor Counties cricket for Lincolnshire: They were Alfred Everson Harrisson and John Carter Harrisson. See for example the *Stamford Mercury* 14 August 1891 and 20 November 1891.

Page 5: sometimes played with his son-in-law: e.g., *Bedfordshire Times and Independent* 29 June 1934.

Page 5: Frank himself won the St Neots Golf Club's Steward's Cup in 1929: *http://421.preview.csiwebsites.com/page.aspx?pid=47129* (accessed 20 April 2022).

Page 5: George captained the St Neots' golfers: e.g., *Bedfordshire Times and Independent* 12 June 1936.

Page 5: **to take part in the 1946 English Amateur Championship:** *Yorkshire Post* 30 April 1946.

Page 5: **He played cricket alongside Frank Crossley and Lord Malden:** *Bedfordshire Times and Independent* 3 August 1928.

Page 6: **George Orwell described this group:** The description is in *England Your England*, the first part of *The Lion and the Unicorn: Socialism and the English Genius* by George Orwell (1941).

Page 6: **their chestnut gelding Flash:** 'Class 19. – Open: Hack of hunter type, over 14.2 hands; 1 Mrs. J. F. Crossley, Riseley, chestnut gelding Flash', *Bedfordshire Times and Independent* 29 June 1928.

Page 6: **Oakley Hunt is known to have met at least once at The Mallowry:** 'Hunting Appointments' in *Bucks Herald* 8 February 1929.

Page 6: **Frank won numerous prizes for his fruit, vegetables and flowers:** For example, for his roses, red currants, cooking apples, marrows, onions, turnips, beets, lettuces and cabbages, *Bedfordshire Times and Independent* 5 August 1927. In 1952 he gave his occupation as 'Market Gardener'.

Page 6: **Both Frank and Winnie were good enough to represent Bedfordshire:** Bedfordshire Archives holds a series of photographs of the Bedfordshire County Lawn Tennis teams. Frank appears in the men's team photographs in 1935, 1937 and 1938 (respectively references X769/5/7, X769/5/8 and X769/5/9). Winnie appears in the women's team photographs in 1930, 1933 and circa 1936 (respectively references X769/4/1, X769/4/2 and X769/4/3). The date of 'circa 1936' given to the photograph of the women's team cannot be correct because Winnie was touring with C. W. A. Scott's Flying Display during the summer of 1936. The photograph is most likely to have been taken in 1934 or 1935.

Page 6: **Towards the end of 1932, the Crossleys left Riseley:** For centuries tenancies were usually renewed at Michaelmas (September 29). The *Biggleswade Chronicle* 9 September 1932 carried a notice for a forthcoming sale of surplus household goods, furniture and effects at Old Woodbury belonging the previous tenant, Mr. R. Tyron. In all probability the Crossleys took on the tenancy at Michaelmas 1932. They were certainly living there in 1933 but seem to have retained the lease of their previous home The Mallowry until May 1935 when they sold it for £1,950 (information via Simon Bates).

Part Two: Take-off

Page 8: **Between 1911 and 1927 a total of just nine certificates were issued to women**: A very useful chart of the number of Aviator's Certificates issued by the Royal Aero Club between 1911 and 1934 is can be found on Terry Mace's website about interwar aviation at *www.afleetingpeace.org*

Page 8: **Winnie's future colleague Amy Johnson, her future friend Lois Butler and her future boss Pauline Gower**: Amy Johnson and Lois Butler learned to fly in 1929 (*www.afleetingpeace.org*). Pauline Gower learned to fly in 1930 (Gower, *Women With Wings*).

Page 8: **in an interview she gave to the *Luton News* in 1939**: *Luton News*, 25 May 1939. Like many other reporters, the paper's 'Madge' wrongly claimed that Winnie had flown as an aerobatic pilot with Cobham's display. The interview is illustrated with a rather romantic photograph of Winnie in flying helmet and goggles.

Page 9: **£1 17s. 6d. an hour for dual instruction, and £1 10s. 0d. an hour for solo hire**: *Aeroplane*, 4 April 1934. In *Flight*, 19 April 1934, the Norfolk and Norwich Aero Club announced it was reducing these prices to £1 15s. 0d. an hour for dual and £1 5s. 0d. an hour for solo hire.

Page 10: **an oral technical examination of 60 questions**: The requirements to gain a Royal Aero Club Aviator's Certificate are in Winchester, *Wonders of World Aviation*, Volume I, p350.

Page 10: **a de Havilland Cirrus II Moth**: Information on the Cirrus I Moth and the Cirrus II Moth is from Jackson, *De Havilland Aircraft since 1909*.

Page 11: **joined Marshalls Flying School at Cambridge**: *Flight*, 16 March 1934; she joined the Northamptonshire Aero Club, *Flight*, 27

September 1934; the Bedfordshire School of Flying at Barton appointed her Vice President, *Flight*, 18 August 1938; she was a member of the London Aeroplane Club by 1935, *Flight*, 2 January 1936.

Page 12: **she said she spent almost 400 hours in the air**: *Luton News*, 25 May 1939.

Page 12: **de Havilland DH 60G Gipsy Moth, registered G-AAET**: For the full history of G-AAET see *https://air-britain.com/pdfs/production-lists/DH60.pdf*; G-AAET was built in 1929. While based at Sywell in 1933 it crashed, and a year later it was sold to Mrs. Winifred Mary Crossley, who based the aircraft at Old Warden. After she sold it the aircraft was used mainly as a club machine until it was impressed into the RAF in June 1940. G-AAET was scrapped in 1941.

Page 12: **Old Warden was the private aerodrome of Richard Shuttleworth**: Ogilvy, *Shuttleworth: The Historic Aeroplanes*.

Page 12: **the DH 60G Gipsy Moth Winnie purchased**: Details are taken from Jackson, *De Havilland Aircraft since 1909*.

Page 13: **air-to-air photographs taken of herself at the controls**: Original photographs and postcard in the possession of Diana Scott.

Page 13: **was the charity flying display**: *Bedfordshire Times and Independent*, 21 September 1934.

Page 14: **taking a course in advanced aerobatics**: *Flight*, 27 December 1934.

Page 14: **the headline Woman 'Stunt' Flier**: *Biggleswade Chronicle* 22 March 1935.

Part Three: The Art of Aerobatics

Page 15: **In an interview with a Canadian newspaper**: *Miniota Herald*, 11 April 1946.

Page 15: William Fair, an insurance agent in Kingston, Ontario: Canadian Census for 1871 and 1901.

Page 15: His bride, Sophia Cleugh, (pronounced Clew) was fourteen years his junior: Canadian Census for 1911 and 1921.

Page 15: Howard Fair was an internationally-renowned polo player and horseman: Obituaries in the *Aiken Standard*, 15 September 1987, and *The Philadelphia Inquirer*, 24 September 1987. Howard Fair was a graduate of the Royal Military College in Kingston, Ontario, and served in the British Army with the Royal Horse Artillery. During the Second World War he served in Europe with the Canadian Army. A member of the U.S. Polo Association, he played polo for 40 years and was internationally known as a competitor. He was the first president of the U.S. Pony Club. His first marriage to Marie Hofmann, the daughter of pianist Josef Hofmann, ended in divorce. He then married Cintra Carter, the ex-wife of William Thornton Carter. He was a survivor of the sinking of the Titanic. She committed suicide in 1956. Howard Fair married twice more: his third wife died in 1970, and his fourth wife survived him.

Page 15: Virginia, two years his junior, was a well-known musician and entertainer: See for example *Medicine Hat News*, 27 July 1934, *Winnipeg Free Press*, 28 December 1939.

Page 15: Arnold, who joined the Royal Canadian Mounted Police; Arthur, who became a sergeant-pilot: Interview with Alfred Davidson Colin Cleugh-Fair in the *Montreal Gazette*, 19 August 1941. 'Arnold, better known to the family as "Bud", is a non-commissioned officer with the Royal Canadian Mounted Police in British Columbia'. 'Arthur... is now a sergeant pilot in the Royal Canadian Air Force, stationed at Moncton, N.B.'.

Page 15: Peter was born in Kingston in 1906: On 18 May 1906: Frontenac, Kingston, Ontario Birth Register; 1939 Register, Bristol.

Page 15: a cadet at the Royal Military College of Canada (RMC): A brief biography and photograph of Peter Fair in the *Royal Military College of Canada Review*, June 1927, also contains the information that 'he plays the piano and is one of the mainstays of the Orchestra'.

Page 16: **He duly crossed the Atlantic in 1927**: On the *Empress of Scotland*, from Quebec to Southampton, arriving 2 November 1927. (Ship's Passenger List, via *www.ancestry.co.uk*).

Page 16: **By May 1928 he had been promoted to the rank of Flying Officer**: *The London Gazette*, 11 December 1928.

Page 16: **He was sent to Malta in 1929**: *https://www.rafweb.org/Members%20Pages/Unit%20Details/Fleet_Air_Arm/446%20Flt.htm*

Page 16: **In 1931 he was with (No 1) Coast Defence Co-operation/Training Flight**: *https://www.rafweb.org/Members%20Pages/Unit%20Details/Misc_flying/CD_Co-op_%20Flt.htm* (accessed 3 May 2019).

Page 16: **promotion to Flight Lieutenant came in 1933**: *The London Gazette*, 1 August 1933.

Page 16: **Flying Officer Fair was among a number of RAF officers presented**: *Flight*, 6 March 1931.

Page 16: **Some of Peter's leisure time was taken up with playing ice hockey**: His career as an ice hockey player can be found in *Lion In Winter: A Complete Record of Great Britain at the Olympic, World and European Ice Hockey Championships 1910–1981*, by David S Gordon and Martin C Harris (British Ice Hockey Heritage Publications, 2019).

Page 16: **A photograph of the Wembley Canadians team in full gear**: *https://i.pinimg.com/originals/f6/28/d8/f628d8ffb5bd149dbc760e0272ca6319.jpg* (accessed 3 May 2019).

Page 16: **among the visitors to arrive by air**: *Flight*, 4 April 1935.

Page 17: **an air taxi and aircraft hire company called Warden Aviation.** Ogilvy, *Shuttleworth: The Historic Aeroplanes.*

Page 17: **she gave an aerobatic display at the Norfolk and Norwich Aero Club's annual garden party**: *Flight*, 12 September 1935.

Page 17: second in the London Aeroplane Club's forced landing competition and won their aerobatic contest: *Flight*, 19 September 1935. Ranald Porteus (1916-1998) came second in the aerobatic contest: he was later the Chief Test Pilot at Auster Aircraft Ltd.

Page 17: At the opening of Shoreham Airport: *Flight*, 26 September 1935.

Page 17: the Norfolk and Norwich Aero Club's cross-country competition: *Flight*, 17 October 1935.

Page 17: The *Tatler* photographed her at Heston in full flying suit: The *Tatler*, 3 April 1935.

Page 17: She appeared in *The Bystander*: *The Bystander*, 29 May 1935.

Page 17: she collected the London Aeroplane Club's aerobatics trophy: *Flight*, 2 January 1936.

Page 17: At 1.30 a.m. on Thursday 28 November 1935: Dr. Harrisson published a short account of the birth of the quadruplets in the *British Medical Journal*, 21 December 1935, page 1207, and a full account of the care they received during their first nine months of life in the *British Medical Journal*, 7 November 1936, pages 917-920. The *Dundee Courier*, 29 November 1935, described Dr. Harrisson as 'this country doctor, grey-haired, fresh complexioned, and bespectacled'.

Page 18: Daily air trips to supply the babies: For example, *Dundee Evening Telegraph*, 2 December 1935.

Page 18: milk supplies from London were augmented from a hospital in Bedford: *British Medical Journal*, 7 November 1936, page 918.

Page 19: an oxygen tent was to be flown by air ambulance: *Gloucestershire Echo*, 2 December 1935.

Page 19: the *Daily Mirror's* lead story: *Daily Mirror*, 29 November 1935.

Page 19: **Dr. Harrisson's wife admitted to a reporter**: *Gloucestershire Echo*, 29 November 1935.

Page 19: **Daily bulletins on their progress were posted on the gates**: One of the bulletins appears in the newsreel made of the quadruplets at Christmas 1935, which can be seen at: *https://www.britishpathe.com/video/VLVAEP8OUAJK109C3NAW6XMQU02WK-TAKING-CARE-OF-THE-FAMOUS-QUADRUPLETS/query/st+neots+quads* (accessed 20 January 2020).

Page 19: **The King sent a cheque for £4**: Such a gift was known as the King's Bounty, given to the parents of triplets or quads. The payment was widely reported in the newspapers, for example by the *Dundee Evening Telegraph*, 2 December 1935. A photograph of the cheque can be seen at *www.stneotsmuseum.org.uk/articles/surviving-the-odds-the-story-of-the-st-neots-quads/* (accessed 9 December 2021).

Page 19: **The newsreels were quickly off the mark**: British Medical Journal, 7 November 1936, page 918.

Page 19: **Gaumont's publicity manager, Hugh Findlay, lived at Havelock House in Gamlingay**: My father remembered the family very well. In 1936 Hugh Findlay invited the Gaumont British studio football team down to play Gamlingay Football Club, a game the home team lost 7-0: *The Era*, 15 April 1936. The family were still there in 1939 (1939 Register, *findmypast.co.uk* accessed 15 June 2022), by which time Hugh Findlay had left Gaumont British and joined New World Pictures: *Kinematograph Yearbook 1942*, (Kinematograph Publications Ltd., London, 1942) page 251.

Page 20: **The parents were filmed walking up the drive**: The conversation recorded by Gaumont British between the doctor and the humble parents when they arrive at The Shrubbery is very revealing. Dr. Harrisson shakes hands with them, and says 'How do you do? Very pleased to see you, and I want to thank you very much indeed for the presents you and Mr. Miles have sent us, and I hope, by way of return, to introduce you to your babies, whom you haven't seen since they were born.'

Mrs. Miles: Thank you very much, and that's the nicest present you could give me.

Dr. Harrisson: And I'm looking forward to the time when we shall be able to get a house big enough to house you and your family together

Mrs. Miles: Thank you very, very much indeed.

Part Four: Circus Performer

Page 21: *Flight* carried a paragraph stating that a new aviation company: *Flight*, 26 December 1935.

Page 21: **Charles William Anderson Scott**: C. W. A. Scott (1903-1946) learned to fly with the RAF. In 1926 he emigrated to Australia and became an airline pilot. He broke the England-Australia solo flight record in 1931, for which he received the Air Force Cross. In 1934 he and Tom Campbell Black received the £10,000 prize for winning the England-Australia MacRobertson Air Race. In 1946, in a state of depression, he killed himself. (*https://www. outlived.org/person/c-w-a-scott-64136* accessed 15 November 2022).

Page 21: **a specially-designed twin-engine de Havilland DH 88 Comet**: Three DH 88 Comets were designed and built by de Havilland for the 1934 MacRobertson Air Race. Featuring long, thin, tapering wings and underslung 230 hp engines, the graceful, streamlined Comet could cruise at 220 mph for long distances. Scott and Campbell Black's winning aircraft, the red and white Comet G-ACSS, survives with the Shuttleworth Collection at Old Warden, Bedfordshire, and is still airworthy. (Ogilvy, *Shuttleworth: The Historic Aeroplanes*.)

Page 21: **Joan Meakin, a skilled glider pilot**: One of the leading glider pilots of the inter-war years, in 1934 Joan Meakin (1910-1977) became the first female glider pilot to fly over the English Channel. She had toured with Cobham's flying display during 1935. (*http://nother.us/joan-meakin-glider-pilot/* accessed 28 April 2022).

Page 21: **Captain Percival Phillips**: For Captain Phillips' extraordinary career in aviation, see Chapman, *Cornwall Aviation Company*.

Page 22: **de Havilland DH 82A Tiger Moth G-ADWG**: One of the greatest trainers ever built, the Tiger Moth first flew in 1931. Well over 8,000 had been built by the time production ceased in 1945. The main production variant of the Tiger Moth - the DH 82A - appeared in 1934 with a 130 hp de Havilland Gipsy Major engine, which gave it a top speed of just over 100 m.p.h. It cruised at 90 m.p.h. and had a range of 300 miles. Winnie was to spend many hundreds of hours flying Tiger Moths. (Jackson, *De Havilland Aircraft since 1909*). Most of the early Tiger Moths were built for the services and training organisations, but a handful were released for civilian use. Scott's company was allowed to purchase G-ADWG new in March 1936. After the tour ended it was sold to the Cinques Ports Flying Club at Lympne in Kent and repainted.

Page 22: **Winnie must have had her 'B' Licence, the professional pilot's licence**: To obtain a 'B' Licence the pilot must have completed 100 hours of solo flying. The practical flying tests to be passed included general flying and spinning. Two cross-country flights of at least 200 miles had to be made, one of them a triangular flight with two stops which had to include an hour flown at a height of 6,500 feet. The other cross-country flight was made with an examiner in the aircraft, and included three forced landings. The pilot also had to make a night flight of at least 30 minutes, and a flight by instruments alone. A theory test and a stiff medical examination were also required (*Wonders of World Aviation*, Volume I, page 459). According to Lettice Curtis in an article about the ATA (*Anything To Anywhere*, published in *Aeroplane Monthly*, February 1979) the 'First Eight' women pilots selected at the end of 1939 for the ATA were 'all qualified instructors'. Winnie herself said that before the war she had 'an instructor's licence' (*Maniota Herald*, 11 April 1946).

Page 22: **The press release sent to local newspapers**: Many local newspapers simply used the press release virtually word-for-word, for example *Londonderry Sentinel*, 2 June 1936, and *Hastings and St. Leonards Observer*, 18 July 1936.

Page 22: **The *Wells Journal* named her their *Woman of the Week***: *Wells Journal*, 1 May 1936.

Page 22: **'The First Woman Aerobatic Pilot'**: *Fife Free Press*, 4 July 1936.

Page 22: **the first woman to demonstrate aerobatics**: *Flight*, 16 April 1936.

Page 23: 'a **Guinness a day helped her to stand the strain of daily aerobatic flights**': Chapman, *Cornwall Aviation Company*, page 56.

Page 23: **A limited number of free flights were given to local newspapers:** For instance, the *Derby Evening Telegraph* of 6 May 1936 reported that it was given 40 tickets for free flights; two of the recipients were taken up by Winnie. By contrast, the *Kirkintilloch Herald* said in its 8 July 1936 issue that it had been given 'half-a-dozen free flights'.

Page 23: **The 'Aero Show Marquee':** *Flight*, 16 April 1936.

Page 23: **The show opened with a massed flypast of aircraft:** *Flight*, 16 April 1936.

Page 24: **the Ace of Spades' airfield at Hook, to the southwest of London:** (*https://www.abct.org.uk/airfields/airfield-finder/hook/* accessed 13 August 2019)

Page 24: **it was a combination of filling station, garage, café restaurant and nightclub:** In 1933 an advertisement in the *Illustrated London News* for the Ace of Spades promised a cafe restaurant, dance club, club terrace, a new swimming pool, garage workshops and fuel. And it was open all night. (*https://www.agefotostock.com/age/en/details-photo/advertisement-for-the-ace-of-spades-road-house-on-the-kingston-by-pass-considered-the-first-of-its-kind-road-houses-sprang-up-along-arterial-roads-leading-out/MEV-12548430* accessed 6 January 2022)

Page 24: **In 1933 the owners acquired a small grass field:** *Flight*, 6 July 1933.

Page 24: **photographed perched on the fuselage:** (*https://www.gettyimages.co.uk/detail/news-photo/aerobatic-pilot-winifred-crossley-getting-into-the-cockpit-news-photo/3067246* accessed 21 June 2022)

Page 24: **a rug in front of the diminutive Hillson-Praga Air Baby:** (*www.alamy.com* accessed 13 August 2019)

Page 24: **Registered as G-ADXL and painted a vivid yellow all over:** *British Civil Aircraft Since 1919*, Volume Three, by A. J. Jackson (Second Edition, Putnam, London, 1974).

Page 24: the display on 12 April at New Barnet: The photographs are at www.*alamy.com*.

Page 24: actors Aileen Marson and Billy Milton: Aileen Marson (1912–1939) was a British stage and screen actress, starring in a number of leading roles in British films during the 1930s. She died at the age of 26 after giving birth to twins (*https://www.imdb.com/name/nm0551320/bio* accessed 28 April 2022, and *https://en.wikipedia.org/wiki/Aileen_Marson* accessed 28 April 2022). Born in Paddington, London, Billy Milton (1905–1989) was an actor, composer and writer (*https://www.imdb.com/name/nm0590652/* accessed 28 April 2022). In 1936 he and Aileen Marson starred in the thriller *Someone At The Door*.

Page 24: attended that first display: *Flight*, 16 April 1936.

Page 25: pilots H. A. Shotter and L. J. Rimmer: Little is known of H. A. Shotter, save that he was a Pilot Officer in the R.A.F. 1929-30 (*Flight*, 4 April 1929 and 23 May 1930) and a joy-riding pilot with C. W. A. Scott's flying display (*Flight*, 16 April 1936). Lancelot John Rimmer, a Canadian who came over with the Canadian Expeditionary Force in the First World War, was a leading joy-riding pilot between the wars, flying with both Cobham and Scott. During the Second World War he became a Halifax test pilot. (Cruddas, *Those Fabulous Flying Years*, page 111.)

Page 25: Idwal Jones: Aerobatic pilot touring with both Cobham and Scott's air displays, known as 'The Wizard of the Air'. Killed in an aircraft crash in 1937. (Cruddas, *Those Fabulous Flying Years*, page 110.)

Page 25: Ronald Ashley: Ronald J Ashley was an autogiro pilot who had flown with Cobham in 1935. He gained his Aviator's Certificate in 1934. (*https://www.flickr.com/photos/7691137@N06/4623778146/in/photostream/* accessed 29 April 2022). 'He learnt to fly an Autogiro before he could fly an aeroplane' (*Waterford Standard*, 16 May 1936.). This was at Hanworth aerodrome in Middlesex, where he 'had been one of the best pupils at the Autogiro School' (*33 Squadron RAF Newsletter*, Issue 8, Summer 2018, page 31, 'Extracts from Spitfires & Autogiros: A History of Upper Culham Farm, by Darren J. Pitcher'). After touring with C. W. A. Scott in 1936 Ashley joined the British Overseas Airways Corporation (BOAC) and flew with them throughout the war. He became the personal pilot of BOAC's director Air Commodore A. C. Critchley, and Critchley, along with Cobham and Ashley, set up an airline in 1946 called Skyways. Cobham, who could see the way the wind was blowing, resigned from Skyways a few months later. The airline struggled on for five years before collapsing. (Cruddas, *Sir Alan Cobham*, pages 170-171.)

Page 26: **Martin Hearn's wingwalking act**: Martin Hearn (1906-1992). Fearless wingwalker who appeared with Cobham's and with Scott's air displays. Set up his own aeronautical engineering business in 1937. (Cruddas, *Those Fabulous Flying Years*, page 109.)

Page 26: **the show moved on to the next venue at Chesham**: The itinerary for the 1936 season has been recreated as far as it can be from local newspaper advertisements, reports, photographs and other sources including the partial itinerary in Cruddas, *Those Fabulous Flying Years*, pages 122-123.

Page 26: **'drove people into the marquees for shelter'**: *Shepton Mallet Journal*, 17 April 1926.

Page 26: **Flight Lieutenant Tommy Rose made an appearance**: *Western Daily Press*, 30 April 1936.

Page 27: **made a personal appearance**: *Kinematograph Weekly*, 14 October 1936.

Page 27: **a wingtip touched the ground**: 'Mr. Idwal Jones, who was flying solo, was unhurt, but both wingtips on one side of the aeroplane were damaged. The pilot was endeavouring to pelt clowns with flour-bag "bombs", and a wingtip touched the ground as the machine tilted'. *Derby Evening Telegraph*, 7 May 1936.

Page 27: **The newsreel cameras were present at Phoenix Park**: The newsreel can be seen at *https://www.britishpathe.com/video/irish-aviation-day* (accessed 13 August 2019). The report in the *Irish Times* on the display appeared on 11 May 1936.

Page 27: **a snapshot of Winnie and Captain Phillips**: Chapman, *Cornwall Aviation Company*, page 70.

Page 28: the anonymous author of a rather camp weekly gossip column: *Waterford Standard*, 16 May 1936.

Page 28: the Air Ministry deemed the field unsuitable: Letter from C. W. A. Scott published in the *Derbyshire Times*, 3 July 1936, which said 'In the winter the field which we proposed to use was passed by our pilot. A fortnight ago we took the precaution of securing the further opinion from an independent "B" License [sic] pilot, who also authorised the ground as fit for flying. On the afternoon of the day before we were due there, i.e., Wednesday afternoon, an Air Ministry representative insisted upon seeing the ground, and was specially flown there by ourselves. For some reason he refused to give his sanction to this field.' Scott added that the field had been used before without any 'serious difficulties', and pointed out 'the heavy financial loss which we have suffered'.

Page 29: the 'celebrated woman aviatrix': Winnie appeared in Liverpool in the Houghton Restaurant of G. H. Lee and Co. Ltd., Basnett Street. *Liverpool Echo*, 22 June 1936.

Page 29: 'large crowds in spite of the unfavourable weather': *Aberdeen Press and Journal*, 9 July 1936.

Page 29: Despite the rain and the mud: 'Overcast skies and intermittent showers failed to damp the enthusiasm of the 5,000 people who visited the fete at Bretton Park.' *Yorkshire Post*, 20 July 1936.

Page 29: Hastings, Sussex, where bad weather led to the show being abandoned: 'Owing to bad flying conditions yesterday (Friday) Mr. C. W. A. Scott's flying display, which was to have taken place at Church Farm, Fairlight, was abandoned'. *Hastings and St Leonard's Observer*, 1 August 1936.

Page 29: the ground crew and all the equipment set off: The fatal lorry crash and the consequent opening and adjourning of the inquest was reported in the *North Devon Journal*, 20 August 1936, and by the *Western Morning News*, 18 August 1936. The resumed inquest was covered by the *North Devon Journal*, 27 August 1936.

Page 29: 'the shapeless mass of twisted metal and wood work': *North Devon Journal*, 20 August 1936.

Page 29: **standing among the wreckage**: Chapman, *Cornwall Aviation Company*, page 70.

Page 30: **the show still had to go on**: Gower, *Women with Wings*, page 122. Gower says of the death of a parachutist during the 1933 British Hospitals Air Pageant tour, 'in the air-circus business there is no time for sentiment . . .'

Page 30: **chose to head its report** *Clifton Air Display - No Untoward Incidents*: *Halifax Evening Courier*, 24 August 1936.

Page 30: **Flying the Autogiro, Ronald Ashley left Blackpool**: Under the headline 'Thick Fog Holds Up Flying Display - Machines Delayed In Reaching Belfast - Difficulty In Crossing Irish Sea', the *Northern Whig*, 2 September 1936, carried details of the arrival of Ronald Ashley and Captain Phillips.

Page 30: **Mr Scott's daring pilots**: *Belfast News-Letter*, 3 September 1936.

Page 30: **In Ballymena the local paper said of Winnie**: *Ballymena Weekly*, 12 September 1936.

Page 31: **Harry Ward, who claimed to be Britain's only 'bird-man'**: *Birmingham Daily Gazette*, 21 September 1936.

Page 31: **Scott's friend Tom Campbell Black**: Thomas Campbell Black (1899-1936) had learned to fly in the Royal Naval Air Service in 1917. He became famous overnight when with C. W. A. Scott he won the 1934 MacRobertson Air Race from Mildenhall to Melbourne in a de Havilland DH 88 Comet. In 1936 he headed up the British Empire Air Display, a smaller display than Scott's which also toured the country giving joy-rides. Campbell Black was among the contestants in an air race to South Africa in late September 1936 but died at a publicity event at Liverpool a few days before the race was due to begin. His friend C. W. A. Scott and co-pilot Giles Guthrie won the race in a Percival Vega Gull and the £10,000 prize. (*https://en.wikipedia.org/wiki/Tom_Campbell_Black* accessed 15 November 2020)

Page 31: £150 in cash, the box-office takings for the day's display: *Birmingham Daily Gazette*, 25 September 1936.

Page 31: In her book *Women With Wings*: Gower, *Women with Wings*, page 178.

Page 31: would visit more than 150 sites: *Flight*, 16 April 1936.

Page 32: a receiver was appointed: Chapman, *Cornwall Aviation Company*, page 56.

Page 32: the company saying in a statement: *Aberdeen Press and Journal*, 3 November 1936.

Part Five: The Show Goes On

Page 33: In 1935 Captain Phillips had set up a company called Air Publicity Ltd: Chapman, *Cornwall Aviation Company*, page 72.

Page 33: His fleet consisted of eight Avro 504Ns: Air Publicity's aircraft are listed in Chapman, *Cornwall Aviation Company*, page 86.

Page 33: The company manufactured its own banners on-site at Heston: Details of the banners, how they were towed, how the aircraft operated away from base and examples of what they advertised are in Chapman, *Cornwall Aviation Company*, pages 72-73, and *Vintage Aircraft* magazine No. 17, July-September 1980, pages 8-11.

Page 33: She was the only female pilot on the staff: Chapman, *Cornwall Aviation Company*, page 74.

Page 33: Her first banner-towing assignment was over Luton: *Luton News*, 25 May 1939. 'All the week Mrs. Crossley is flying from one large town in England to another, to spend the day trailing her advertising slogans above the rooftops of Manchester, Birmingham and other big cities . . . Mrs. Crossley has only flown over Luton once on an advertising campaign. That was when she started commercial flying about three years ago, and Luton was her first consignment [sic]'.

Page 34: **found herself flying backwards over Sauchiehall Street**: Chapman, *Cornwall Aviation Company*, page 74.

Page 34: **as a local newspaper noted, 'the fog thickened'**: *Walsall Observer*, 25 December 1937.

Page 34: **The Government were the target of one banner**: *Yorkshire Post*, 23 July 1937.

Page 34: **describing his job as one of the most boring in aviation**: Chapman, *Cornwall Aviation Company*, page 74.

Page 35: **could tow seven gliders in succession to 2,000 feet**: Chapman, *Cornwall Aviation Company*, page 74.

Page 35: **On Coronation Day 1937, flying a hired Tiger Moth**: *Biggleswade Chronicle*, 21 May 1937. 'Mrs. Crossley used a D.H. Tiger Moth, which was specially chartered for the occasion.'

Page 35: **the RAF's No. 1 Armoured Car Company**: In 1935 the unit was staffed by two squadron leaders, four flight lieutenants, three flying officers and three pilot officers. Peter Fair was still on strength in July 1936. *https://www.rafweb.org/Members%20Pages/Unit%20Details/Misc_non-flying/AAC-1.htm* (accessed 27 April 2022)

Page 35: **a change in his wife's attitude towards him during 1935**: *Kent & Sussex Courier*, 29 October 1937.

Page 36: **The *Daily Mirror* said the adultery took place 'at a camp in Iraq'**: *Daily Mirror*, 27 October 1937. The National Archives holds the court records, reference Divorce Court File: 4385. Appellant: Laurence Barton Grafftey-Smith. Respondent: Vivien Isabel Grafftey-Smith. Co-respondent: Peter Cleugh Fair.

Page 36: **Peter Fair had left the RAF at his own request**: *London Gazette*, 13 April 1937: 'Flight Lieutenant Peter Cleugh FAIR is placed on the retired list at his own request. 8 Apr. 1937.'

SOURCES

Page 36: banner towing in Avro 504N G-ACRE over Hull and Grimsby: The inquest into the death of Captain Phillips and the events leading up to the fatal crash were reported in the *Cornish Guardian*, 17 February 1938, the *Bedfordshire Times and Independent*, 18 February 1938, and the *Biggleswade Chronicle*, 18 February 1938.

Page 36: buzzing the White Horse Inn at Eaton Socon: Chapman, *Cornwall Aviation Company*, page 75.

Page 36: Winnie had decided to leave Frank and marry Peter Fair: By the author in Chapman, *Cornwall Aviation Company*, page 75. No source is given for this statement, nor for Captain Phillips' buzzing the pub in Eaton Socon and following Winnie's car back to Old Woodbury at hedgetop level, or that Winnie said he was in 'a naughty mood' that day. Perhaps Winnie had written to the Captain's family after the crash and Chapman was quoting from her letter. The author suggested that Phillips was upset by the possibility of Winnie getting a divorce, and that his flying judgement may have been affected by the news. If such a thing was discussed, I doubt it would have had any effect on his flying judgement.

Page 37: Peter Fair was an experienced pilot: Fair said Phillips' take off was made 'in the normal manner into a very strong wind. He climbed to about 200 feet, did a left-hand turn and came back across the field. He had lost some height in turning and was carried by the excessively strong wind in such a manner as to prevent him avoiding a high tree at the end of the field. The impact threw the machine out of control, causing it to crash to the ground about 100 yards further on'. *Biggleswade Chronicle*, 18 February 1938.

Page 37: a photograph of the skeletal remains of G-ACRE: It appeared in the *Cambridge Independent Press*, 18 February 1938.

Page 37: Winnie said it was her 'most awful day': Chapman, *Cornwall Aviation Company*, page 75.

Page 37: *Flight*'s short obituary: *Flight*, 17 February 1938.

Page 37: **he was never happier than when he was in the air**: *Cornish Guardian*, 17 February 1938.

Page 37: ***Sailplane and Glider's* obituary said**: 'His handling of his "Avro 504" was masterly, and no one but he was capable of towing up sailplanes from the club ground at Dunstable in safety in all weathers. He was to have done most of the towing at the forthcoming Leicester meeting, but his place will now be taken by Mrs. Crossley'. *Sailplane and Glider*, Volume 9, number 3, March 1938.

Page 38: **the dozen or so gliders were towed by Winnie**: 'The gliders, of which there were about a dozen – chiefly Grunau 'planes – were towed from the ground by an Avro machine flown by Mrs. Winifred Crossley, and released at 2,000 feet.' *Leicester Evening Mail*, 16 April 1938.

Page 38: **they left Birmingham to fly to Yeadon**: The story was headlined 'PILOTED BY WOMAN – Plane Forced Down in Bradford – Thrill For Bierley Residents'. *Yorkshire Observer*, 24 June 1938.

Page 39: **With her was Captain Phillips' spaniel Kim**: *The Scotsman*, 15 July 1938:

Page 39: **Winnie spent the week towing gliders from the nearby private airfield**: The gliders were all 'towed up to 2,000 feet by aeroplane from Studham, the private aerodrome of Mr. Alan Butler'. *The Scotsman*, 15 July 1938. A photograph, taken from the passenger seat of Winnie's Avro looking back over the tail, showing a Cambridge University Club glider being towed aloft, appeared in *Flight*, 21 July 1938.

Page 39: **Romford Flying Club set up the National Women's Air Reserve**: *Brentwood & Ongar Gazette*, 29 July 1988, in a feature called 'From The Files 50 Years Ago'.

Page 40: **aerobatic display in one at Cardiff airport**: 'While they waited, Mrs. Winifred Crossley went up to give an impromptu, but nevertheless polished demonstration of aerobatics in a London Aeroplane Club Tiger. Soon after her excellent show was over the Chilton was sighted, well on its course.' *Flight*, 15 September 1938.

Page 40: she performed at the Civic Air Day at Norwich: *Flight*, 10 November 1938.

Page 40: Winnie had two engine failures while flying the old Avros: Chapman, *Cornwall Aviation Company*, page 74.

Page 40: she was towing a banner over 100,000 people: *Nottingham Evening Post*, 1 May 1939.

Page 40: PLANE NEARLY FELL INTO CUP FINAL: *Newcastle Evening Chronicle*, 1 May 1939.

Page 40: Trouble Over Cup Final - Woman Pilot's Coolness: *Dundee Courier*, 1 May 1939.

Page 40: According to the *Biggleswade Chronicle*'s **account:** 'FORCED LANDING ON GOLF COURSE', *Biggleswade Chronicle*, 5 May 1939. The *Luton News*, 25 May 1939, said 'When she came down on a golf course recently she was reported as "stepping calmly from the plane and remarking 'sorry chaps, can I have a cigarette?'" "Naturally I felt quite shaky and said nothing of the kind," Mrs. Crossley told me, although she did apologise for stopping the game.'

Page 40: Frank Crossley gave in his notice: Waresley Estate correspondence in Bedfordshire Archives, reference PM2939/1/2/20.

Page 40: commissioned in the Royal Artillery in June: Bedfordshire Archives, reference Z910/1/4.

Page 40: head-and-shoulders portrait of Winnie: In the possession of Winnie's niece Penelope Cheshire.

Page 41: the banners Winnie towed now were aimed at recruiting people: 'Recently the slogans behind her plane have been mainly recruiting publicity for National Service.' *Luton News*, 25 May 1939.

Page 41: one last aerobatic display, at Redhill: *Flight*, 3 August 1939.

Part Six: Anything To Anywhere

Page 42: In 1938 Captain Peter Fair won an award: He was one of four pilots awarded the Reliability Trophy of the Guild of Air Pilots and Air Navigators. *Birmingham Mail*, 23 December 1939.

Page 42: he was flying on the Berlin, Warsaw and Stockholm routes: *Birmingham Mail*, 23 December 1939.

Page 42: the commander of a Lockheed Super Electra: *aviation-safety. net/database/record.php?id=19391221-0* (accessed 3 May 2019).

Page 42: There were eleven people on board: five crew and six passengers: *Sheffield Daily Telegraph*, 23 December 1939.

Page 42: The aircraft made a scheduled stop at Sollum: *Leicester Daily Mercury*, 23 December 1939.

Page 42: It made a routine radio call to Malta at 10.20 a.m.: *Sheffield Daily Telegraph*, 23 December 1939.

Page 42: A search and rescue mission was launched: *The People*, 24 December 1939.

Page 42: it was a French ship, the *St Georges*: *Birmingham Mail*, 23 December 1939.

Page 42: Only six men survived the ditching: The three crew members who survived were Captain Peter Fair, Flight Engineer J. J. Broome and Flight Steward W. Smith. Broome was seriously injured, Fair and Smith 'suffered lesser injuries'. First Officer J. W. F. Beach and Radio Officer G. R. Brentnall died. The surviving passengers were Wing Commander W. L. Dawson, RAF, Lieutenant W. Ashton, RN and Major Mackenson. All the mail on board was lost. *The People*, 24 December 1939, and *www.rcawsey. co.uk/Accmisc.htm* (accessed 3 May 2019). The *Sheffield Daily Telegraph*, 23 December 1939, reassured its worried readers that 'it is understood that no notable personages were on board'.

Page 42: the Captain, Peter Fair, who suffered a broken arm: *Montreal Gazette*, 19 August 1941.

Page 43: eight leading female pilots had been recruited: Virtually every newspaper in the land seems to have carried the story, for example the *Evening Despatch*, 23 December 1939 ('They Will Work "Air Ferry" Service').

Page 43: On her ATA application form: The RAF Museum hold Winnie's ATA records, ATA/1906-01-09/CrossleyW. I am indebted to Terry Mace for generously sending me the photographs he took of the contents of her file. I have quoted extensively from those records here, and any statement about Winnie's time in the ATA not separately referenced is based on them.

Page 43: the brainchild of Gerard d'Erlanger: Cheesman, *Brief Glory*, pages 11.

Page 43: In August 1939 he put forward his idea: Cheesman, *Brief Glory*, page 12.

Page 43: Pauline Gower, the daughter of an M.P., a barnstormer: Cheesman, *Brief Glory*, pages 71; King, *Golden Wings*, page 16.

Page 43: A dozen women were selected: King, *Golden Wings*, pages 16–17, Lettice Curtis, *Anything To Anywhere*, in *Aeroplane Monthly*, February 1979.

Page 44: She had been a qualified flying instructor for at least a year: *The Bystander*, 1 February 1939.

Page 44: The others chosen were: Cheesman, *Brief Glory*, page 73; King, *Golden Wings*, pages 16–17.

Page 44: paraded before the press at de Havilland's Hatfield aerodrome: The story and the photographs were widely reproduced in newspapers and magazines, for example in the *Dundee Courier*, 12 January 1940, and *The Bystander*, 17 January 1940.

Page 44: The Women's Section had its own uniform: Whittell, *Spitfire Women*, page 95; Volkersz, *The Sky and I*, page 38; Wheeler, *The Hurricane Girls*, pages 59-60.

Page 44: pick up their parachutes and run: Whittell, *Spitfire Women*, pages 62-63. The author has mistakenly assumed a later photograph of the ATA women on the patio outside one of Hatfield's buildings was taken this day.

Page 44: Winnie told a reporter: *Daily Mirror*, 11 January 1940.

Page 45: headlines like *Air Girls Go Into 'Action'* and *Women Pilots Aid The RAF*: Respectively in the *Birmingham Daily Gazette*, 11 January 1940, and the *Birmingham Mail*, 11 January 1940.

Page 45: The *Daily Mirror* excelled itself: *Daily Mirror*, 11 January 1940. The main article was headlined '8 Girls "Show" RAF.', and includes a quote from Mona Friedlander, who, the paper said, drives home in her car every evening when off duty. "Then I generally go straight to bed if I'm too tired for a party"'. It also revealed of the women that 'They have an armchair in their rest room, can smoke and make up as much as they please.'

Page 45: Ironically, in his 'Cassandra' column in the next day's *Daily Mirror*: William Connor's outburst is in the *Daily Mirror*, 12 January 1940.

Page 46: as the *Daily Mail* claimed not so long ago: *https://www.dailymail.co.uk/femail/article-3194754/The-female-Guns-World-War-II-Inside-RAF-s-woman-ferry-squadron-rubbed-shoulders-men-flew-Spitfires.html* (accessed 7 May 2022).

Page 46: neither were they the female air force who once ruled our skies: Wheeler, *The Hurricane Girls*, (blurb).

Page 46: the women who dared to fly: Wheeler, *The Hurricane Girls*, (subtitle).

Page 46: using a combination of the quarter-inch Ordnance Survey maps: Lettice Curtis, *Anything To Anywhere*, article in *Aeroplane Monthly*, April 1979.

Page 46: Winnie herself said after the war that most of the ATA casualties: *Miniota Herald*, 11 April 1946.

Page 46: more than 8,000 aircrew died in training and non-operational accidents: *www.iwm.org.uk/history/life-and-death-in-bomber-command* (accessed 7 May 2022).

Page 46: They were not supposed to take-off unless: Whittell, *Spitfire Women*, page 209.

Page 46: From February 1940 it took over the ferrying task completely: Cheesman, *Brief Glory*, pages 22-23.

Page 47: 1,250 pilots from 25 nations around the world: *atamuseum.org* (accessed 7 May 2022).

Page 47: Every machine you see in the sky: Cheesman, *Brief Glory*, page 100.

Page 47: totalling at the end a whopping 309,000 aeroplanes: Cheesman, *Brief Glory*, page 246.

Page 47: January 1940 was the coldest month since the previous century: Wheeler, *The Hurricane Girls*, pp 54, 60.

Page 47: Flights had to stick to recognised routes and be undertaken in gaggles: Curtis, *Lettice Curtis*, page 46.

Page 47: Lettice Curtis, an Oxford triple-blue: Whittell, *Spitfire Women*, page 8.

Page 47: a large, rambling Tudor manor house in North Mymms: Curtis, *Lettice Curtis*, page 45. Bidwell's sale brochure when it was sold recently is at *https://media.onthemarket.com/properties/3739755/doc_1_2. pdf* (accessed 7 May 2022).

Page 47: she put up some of the other women pilots: Curtis, *Lettice Curtis*, page 45.

Page 48: **the use of a twin-engine Avro Anson trainer**: Curtis, *Lettice Curtis*, page 46.

Page 48: **women should fly all types of training aircraft**: Cheesman, *Brief Glory*, page 73.

Page 49: **Her logbooks are now kept in the ATA Museum**: *https://atamuseum.org* has a collection of over 140 A.T.A. pilots' logbooks.

Page 49: **Lettice Curtis wrote that because the women were only flying trainers**: Curtis, *Lettice Curtis*, page 48.

Page 49: **On 3 October Hatfield itself was bombed**: Wheeler, *The Hurricane Girls*, pages 99–100; Curtis, *Lettice Curtis*, page 48.

Page 49: **the logbook of Marion Wilberforce**: *https://atamuseum.org*

Page 50: **The new year opened with snow**: Curtis, *Lettice Curtis*, pages 57–58.

Page 50: **Winnie, Joan Hughes and Lettice Curtis were flown in the taxi Rapide**: Curtis, *Lettice Curtis*, pages 57.

Page 50: **Amy Johnson was heading for Prestwick in Scotland**: Whittell, *Spitfire Women*, pages 46–51.

Page 50: **Lettice Curtis wrote that on 9 January 1941**: Curtis, *Lettice Curtis*, page 61.

Page 51: **Winnie was 'dark and attractive . . . gay and very party-minded'**: Volkersz, *The Sky and I*, page 36.

Page 51: **she was 'as dashing and warm-hearted and gay'**: King, *Golden Wings*, page 17.

Page 51: **flights in taxi Rapides and Ansons piloted by Winnie**: Philippa Bennett's logbook, *https://atamuseum.org*

Page 53: **he was photographed in the middle of a bevy of lady pilots**: The photograph can be seen here: *www.rafmuseum.org.uk/ research/online-exhibitions/americans-in-the-royal-air-force/americans-in-the-british-flying-services-1914-1945/women-pilots/*(accessed 7 May 2022).

Page 53: **Winnie was particularly anxious to get her hands on Hurricanes**: Lettice Curtis, *Anything To Anywhere*, article in *Aeroplane Monthly*, February 1979.

Page 53: **d'Erlanger is said to have remarked to Pauline Gower**: Whittell, *Spitfire Women*, page 111.

Page 53: **Captain R. H. Henderson brought a Hawker Hurricane**: Volkersz, *The Sky and I*, page 43; Curtis, *Lettice Curtis*, page 64; Cheesman, *Brief Glory*, pages 75-76.

Page 54: **With over 2,000 hours to her name**: *Victoria Daily Times*, 15 July 1941.

Page 54: **It was literally with bated breath that we watched Winnie**: King, *Golden Wings*, page 25.

Page 54: **Winnie 'as always did a perfect take-off and landing'**: Volkersz, *The Sky and I*, page 43.

Page 55: **we watched Winnie make the first Hurricane take-off**: King, *Golden Wings*, page 25.

Page 55: **Alison King caught the mood afterwards**: King, *Golden Wings*, page 25.

Page 55: **It was the perfect excuse for a party**: Whittell, *Spitfire Women*, page 112.

Page 55: **ATA pilot Ann Welch wrote about taking a Hurricane to Scotland**: Welch, *Happy to Fly*, page 54.

Page 56: **Alison King claimed one paper published an article**: King, *Golden Wings*, pages 121–122.

Page 56: **30-minute documentary**: *https://www.youtube.com/watch?v= 8fk4mnaz4dU* (accessed 20 January 2020)

Page 56: **Marion Wilberforce, with Winnie Crossley as her second in command**: Curtis, *Lettice Curtis*, page 83.

Page 57: **the incident which took place at RAF Colerne**: The accident reports for all three incidents are available at *www.ata-ferry-pilots.org*

Page 57: **divided the different types of aircraft they flew into six classes**: (*atamuseum.org* accessed 21 June 2020). The classes were: Class 1, light single-engine aircraft - primarily trainers; Class 2, advanced single-engine aircraft - mostly fighters; Class 3, light twin-engine aircraft; Class 4, advanced twin engine aircraft - mostly medium bombers; Class 5, four-engine aircraft - heavy bombers; Class 6, flying boats. Classes 2 and 4 also had plus ratings for more difficult types within that class. Class 2 Plus included P-40 variants, Tempests and Typhoons. Class 4 Plus included Mosquitoes, and twins with tricycle undercarriages such as P-38 Lightnings and B-25 Mitchells.

Page 58: **Captain Geoffrey Wikner**: his account of Winnie's first flight in a Mosquito is in *Flight Of The Halifax: The Biography of Captain G. N. Wikner, Australian Pioneer Aviator*, compiled by Norman Mitchell (published by K. V. Wikner, Australia, 1993) pages 126–127.

Page 58: **it had a fairly high critical speed of 200 mph**: *In the Cockpit: Flying the World's Great Aircraft*, edited by Anthony Robinson (Orbis, London, 1979), pages 161–170.

Page 60: **'a sort of wartime country flying club'**: Cheesman, *Brief Glory*, pages 163–164.

Page 60: **the first woman to fly an RAF four-engine bomber**: Curtis, *Lettice Curtis*, pages 106–112.

Page 61: **women pilots in the ATA had been paid less than male pilots:** Whittell, *Spitfire Women*, page 93.

Page 61: **to persuade the government to give the women equal pay:** Whittell, *Spitfire Women*, page 234.

Page 61: **double-page spread of excellent caricatures:** *The Sketch*, 3 June 1942. 'Sammy' Clayton was Mrs. Edna Clayton, a pilot Third Officer who was in the ATA for a year. Her maiden name was Samuel, hence she was known as 'Sammy'.

Page 62: **Captain Fair flew for BOAC to the Far East and Africa:** *Miniota Herald*, 17 July 1947.

Page 62: **Peter Fair was one of the BOAC pilots who operated the service:** *Montreal Gazette*, 9 September 1944; *Miniota Herald*, 17 July 1947.

Page 62: **Frank, now a major in the Royal Artillery, married again:** *Dundee Courier*, 17 June 1942. His bride was Marie Dring.

Page 62: **'says that his bride-to-be is a better pilot than himself':** *Daily Record*, 9 September 1943. In this report, almost eight years after the event, Winnie was still known as 'the daughter of the late Dr. E. H. Harrisson, who brought the St. Neots quads into the world'.

Page 62: **The marriage took place in London in December 1943:** *Montreal Gazette*, 11 December 1943, says the marriage occurred in London 'yesterday', and has Olive Snell's pastel sketch of Winnie in her uniform (the *Tatler*, 6 October 1943), alongside a head and shoulders photograph of Captain Peter Fair in BOAC uniform and peaked cap.

Page 63: **the best-known photograph of one shows it towering above Joan Hughes:** Cheesman, *Brief Glory*, page 72, and much-reproduced elsewhere.

Page 63: **which featured a tricycle undercarriage:** Until the Second World War most aircraft had two mainwheels beneath the wings and a third, much smaller wheel, located somewhere under the tail. The drawback with this tailwheel arrangement was that it meant the weight of the aircraft's engine (or engines) was ahead of its centre of gravity, which could create difficulties when taxiing, landing or taking off, especially in a crosswind. By positioning a larger third wheel under the nose instead, the weight of the engine was ahead of the centre of gravity and the aircraft was much easier to handle on the ground.

Page 63: **Winnie told a journalist in 1946**: *Miniota Herald*, 11 April 1946.

Page 64: **the ATA staged its final farewell at White Waltham airfield**: Cheesman, *Brief Glory*, pages 207-209; Curtis, *Lettice Curtis*, page 133.

Page 64: **flown '60 different types of military aircraft'**: *Miniota Herald*, 11 April 1946.

Part Seven: Afterwards

Page 67: **By 1947 he had logged 8,500 hours**: *Ottawa Citizen*, 17 July 1947.

Page 67: **visits by air to England**: For instance, Winnie flew from London back to Montreal on 6 November 1951: Passenger manifest, The National Archives via *findmypast.co.uk* (accessed 31 August 2019); London to New York 23 June 1948: Passenger manifest, The National Archives via *findmypast. co.uk* (accessed 15 May 2019).

Page 67: **her son John, a 17-year-old student, crossed the Atlantic**: Passenger manifest, The National Archives via *findmypast.co.uk* (accessed 24 November 2019). He flew from London to New York, 'In transit to Canada' on 11 September 1946.

Page 67: **younger brother Alfred, who called himself Cleugh-Fair**: He was born Alfred Davidson Colin Cleugh Fair in 1913.

Page 68: **Alfred Cleugh-Fair was a line-shooter**: In a revealing interview with the *Montreal Gazette*, 19 August 1941, Squadron Leader A. D. C. Cleugh-Fair confessed that he 'doesn't believe in talking about himself or his achievements'. Not much he didn't. He managed to mention how he had tried his hand at journalism before joining the RAF, and how, after a forced landing he was asked to write up the story for *Blackwood's Magazine* – and it was 'jolly well paid for too'. He had managed to visit his mother and sister, 'but as he puts it, "I'm practically a ruddy Englishman now."' He claimed to be an RAF test pilot, when actually he was an instructor, and that all he wanted was to be allowed 'into the operational end of this war and leave the experimental part to someone else'. Unfortunately he was forced to spend much of the war as a Liaison Officer with the British Air Commission in Washington. Strangely, he didn't mention in the interview how, during the Battle of Britain when he was an instructor at an Operational Training Unit in Cumberland, he had played a large part in the thankfully non-fatal shooting down of a British Armstrong Whitworth Whitley bomber by a Hurricane. The story was recounted in *Aeroplane Monthly*, September 2015, and in *Hurricane 4118 Revisited*, by Peter Vacher (Grub Street, London, 2017).

Page 68: involved in ditching an aeroplane into the sea: 'In September, 1937, he was piloting a flying boat which made a forced landing at sea and there he and the crew were picked up by a Dutch trawler. He recalled how the Dutch sailors lent the fliers wooden sabots, heavy woollen trousers and sweaters all reeking of fish. "As if that wasn't bad enough,' laughed the young pilot, "we had to eat fish all the time we were aboard."

"We landed at Scarborough, England," he continued, "and immediately headed for the Royal Scarborough Hotel, comparable to the Ritz-Carlton (where he stayed while here) in Montreal. We entered the elevator and immediately the rest of the guests got out. They just couldn't stand the smell, and I don't exactly blame them."' (*Montreal Gazette*, 19 August 1941.) It's doubtful if Cleugh-Fair was actually piloting the twin-engine Supermarine Scapa flying boat. According to the *Dundee Courier*, 7 September 1937, the aircraft was commanded by Flight Lieutenant Burgess, the rest of the crew being Pilot Officer Fair (with no Cleugh and no hyphen), a sergeant and three Leading Aircraftsmen. Both engines failed, and after ditching in the sea the Dutch trawler towed the Scapa for eighteen hours through rough seas to Scarborough, sixty miles away. After the war, in 1948, Cleugh-Fair was, like his elder brother, employed in crossing and recrossing the Atlantic – though not as a pilot, but rather as a cabin waiter on the *Queen Mary*.

Page 68: they appeared in the *Tatler*, photographed at a ball: the *Tatler*, 2 April 1952. Chawton is the village where the writer Jane Austen spent the last eight years of her life. Her brother Edward Austen Knight had inherited

Chawton House, a large Elizabethan manor house, and allowed his mother and his sisters Jane and Cassandra to live in a cottage he owned in the village.

Page 68: **Peter had logged over 13,000 flying hours**: *Arizona Republic*, 2 February 1955.

Page 68: **24-year-old Princess Margaret**: *The Guardian*, 7 January 1955, was one among many newspapers that carried the news of his appointment.

Page 68: **The newsreels recorded the departure**: For instance, here: *www. youtube.com/watch?v=B8C-hzc2h8o* (accessed 8 May 2022).

Page 68: **The aircraft refuelled at freezing Montreal**: *Medicine Hat News*, 4 February 1955: 'Crowds who braved sub-zero weather to see Princess Margaret when her plane refuelled at Montreal were disappointed. The Princess did not show herself even at the window, and as the big stratocruiser [sic] took off the crowd groaned. They had chanted "We Want the Princess" as the plane was being refuelled, but only the captain of the ship, Peter Fair of Kingston, Ont., showed himself.'

Page 68: **Peter Fair's landing**: *www.britishpathe.com/video/VLVAE5MX3J L1N22J1P7AJZ3N7OOIU-NEWS/query/Caribbean* (accessed 29 May 2019). This newsreel begins with the refuelling at Montreal and ends with the arrival at Trinidad.

Page 68: **more newsreel cameras**: *www.youtube.com/watch?v=OZ92fE6sWo8* (accessed 8 May 2022).

Page 69: **General Manager of Bahamas Airways Limited**: *Flight*, 3 May 1957.

Page 69: **flew inter-island services and flights**: *Flight*, 3 May 1957.

Page 69: **Ed Ballard, an American who had joined the ATA**: *https:// atamuseum.org* has details of the Ballards' service with the ATA

Page 69: **They were friendly with Lettice Curtis and invited her to stay with them**: Curtis, *Lettice Curtis*, pages 183-185, where she describes the visit in detail.

Page 70: **BOAC sold 80 per cent of its shareholding**: *Flight*, 17 April 1959.

Page 70: **Peter Fair called a press conference**: *Nassau Guardian*, 16 December 1960.

Page 70: **Winnie and Peter had visited England in the summer of 1960**: Passenger manifest, The National Archives, via *Ancestry.co.uk* (accessed 21 August 2019). This is their return journey: their outbound journey from the Bahamas to the UK has not been found.

Page 70: **returned to Nassau on the SS *Reina del Mar***: Passenger manifest, The National Archives, via *Ancestry.co.uk* (accessed 21 August 2019). Their address in the United Kingdom is given as 'C/O Butler, Studham Hall Farm, Nr Dunstable, Beds.' The ship departed from Southampton on 7 July 1960.

Page 70: **died in the Chester County Hospital**: Death certificate of Peter C Fair via *Ancestry.co.uk* (accessed 13 Auguast 2023).

Page 71: **Winnie returned to England**: She flew from Nassau to London via New York in July 1962 (*New York State, Passenger and Crew Lists, 1917-1967*, via *Ancestry.co.uk* accessed 30 September 2023).

Page 71: **took a house called Fox Meadow in Potten End**: Winnie was living there when she made her will in 1978.

Page 71: **a man called Alan Borton**: Information and photograph via Diana Scott. His full name was Edward Alan Borton. A brief biography of him is in *King's College, Cambridge, Annual Report 2008*, page 92. He married Edith Koessler in June 1988 (*England and Wales Marriages, 1837-2005*, via *findmypast.co.uk* (accessed 11 December 2023)). The probate of his will says he died on 30 September 1995 at Tring, Herts., (Probate no: 9651302554, 18 January 1996).

Page 71: **The Swallows in Dagnall**: As recorded in the grant of probate of her will.

Page 71: **She died on 27 March 1984 at the age of 78**: As recorded in the grant of probate of her will.

Page 71: **wished he had married her**: Information via Diana Scott.

Page 72: **Royal Mail issued a set of stamps**: *www.bbc.co.uk/news/uk-england-oxfordshire-61307602* and *www.dailymail.co.uk/news/article-10778619/Royal-Mail-honours-Second-World-Wars-unsung-female-heroes-new-set-stamps.html* (both accessed 26 May 2022).

Page 72: **socialite Diana Barnato Walker**: Whittell, *Spitfire Women*, pages 103–105.

Page 72: **Hertfordshire bus company Uno**: *www.unobus.info/tigermoth-girls/?region=* (accessed 15 November 2021), and also at *https://atamuseum.org/the-flying-buses* (accessed 14 June 2022). I must record my gratitude to the Uno bus company for taking and sending me a photograph of Winnie Crossley's bus.

Page 72: **Barnet Council ran an online poll**: *engage.barnet.gov.uk/name-square-colindale* (accessed 28 April 2022).

Index

Dear Reader,

We hope you have enjoyed this book, but why not share your views on social media? You can also follow our pages to see more about our other products: facebook.com/penandswordbooks or follow us on X @penswordbooks

You can also view our products at www.pen-and-sword.co.uk (UK and ROW) or www.penandswordbooks.com (North America).

To keep up to date with our latest releases and online catalogues, please sign up to our newsletter at: www.pen-and-sword.co.uk/newsletter

If you would like a printed catalogue with our latest books, then please email: enquiries@pen-and-sword.co.uk or telephone: 01226 734555 (UK and ROW) or email: uspen-and-sword@casematepublishers.com or telephone: (610) 853-9131 (North America).

We respect your privacy and we will only use personal information to send you information about our products.

Thank you!